Endorsements

The heart of the gospel is contained in the doctrines of grace. To understand these truths is to understand the height, depth, breadth, and length of the saving grace of God for sinners. Richard Phillips has done an outstanding job of capturing the heartbeat of these precious truths. Prepare your heart to be greatly blessed as this pastor and author guides you into a greater appreciation of the sovereign grace of God.

—DR. STEVEN J. LAWSON
President, OnePassion Ministries, Dallas

Rick Phillips has an unbounded love for the doctrines of grace and writes about them with an enviable simplicity and clarity. Here is persuasive exposition of biblical teaching that captures the thrill of knowing a sovereign God. *What's So Great about the Doctrines of Grace?* never loses sight of the grace to which these doctrines point. This is a wonderful book to read, study, lend, and give away.

—DR. SINCLAIR B. FERGUSON
Professor of systematic theology, Redeemer Seminary, Dallas

Richard Phillips has done it again! In summarizing the doctrines of grace in this book, he brings us into the arena of historic Calvinism, which, as C. H. Spurgeon said, "is the Gospel and nothing else." But what we have here is more than just a retelling of the doctrines themselves; it is an account of why these truths *matter* in the church of the twenty-first century. Its enthusiasm is infectious, its urgency compelling, and its logic irrefutable.

—DR. DEREK W. H. THOMAS
Senior pastor, First Presbyterian Church, Columbia, S.C.

WHAT'S SO GREAT ABOUT THE DOCTRINES OF GRACE?

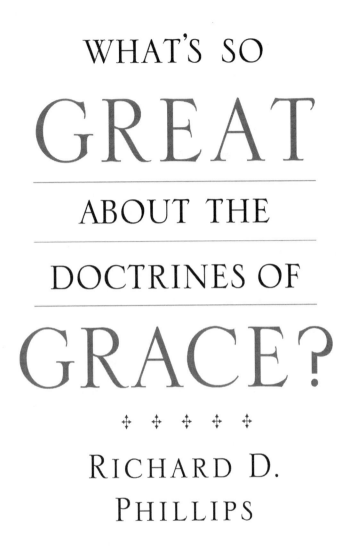

WHAT'S SO
GREAT
ABOUT THE
DOCTRINES OF
GRACE?

✧ ✧ ✧ ✧ ✧

RICHARD D. PHILLIPS

IR *Reformation Trust*   A DIVISION OF LIGONIER MINISTRIES, ORLANDO, FL

What's So Great about the Doctrines of Grace?

© 2008 by Richard D. Phillips

Published by Reformation Trust Publishing
a division of Ligonier Ministries
421 Ligonier Court, Sanford, FL 32771
Ligonier.org   ReformationTrust.com

Printed in Crawfordsville, Indiana
RR Donnelley and Sons
October 2014
First edition, second printing

Cover design: Kirk DouPonce
Interior design and typeset: Katherine Lloyd, The DESK

Unless otherwise indicated, all Scripture quotations are from *The Holy Bible, English Standard Version*, copyright © 2001 by Crossway Bibles, a division of Good News Publishers. Used by permission. All rights reserved.

Scripture quotations marked (NIV) are from the *Holy Bible, New International Version*®. NIV®. Copyright © 1973, 1978, 1984 by International Bible Society. Used by permission of Zondervan. All rights reserved.

Library of Congress Cataloging-in-Publication Data

Phillips, Richard D. (Richard Davis), 1960-
  What's so great about the doctrines of grace? / by Richard D. Phillips.
    p. cm.

 ISBN 1-56769-091-2
 1. Grace (Theology) I. Title.
BT761.3.P45 2008
234--dc22

                                                   2007052749

✤ ✤ ✤

To Chuck and Irene Elliott,
whose lives so beautifully exhibit the sovereign grace of God.

CONTENTS

PREFACE

I LOVE THE DOCTRINES OF GRACE. I love them as *doctrines*, that is, as biblical teachings that are sublime and wonderful beyond all human expectation. There can hardly be thrills greater to the mind than those produced by the central doctrines of the Reformed faith. But I especially love these doctrines because of their marvelous theme: the sovereign *grace* of God for unworthy sinners. For even greater than their enlightening effect on the mind, the doctrines of God are utterly transforming to the believing heart. To love the doctrines of grace is to love God as He has revealed Himself in His Word. He is "the God of all grace" (1 Peter 5:10), and unless we anchor our faith in the fullness of grace taught in Scripture, we will never glorify God for our salvation as He so richly deserves.

This book has two purposes. The first is to explain the doctrines of grace, also known as the "Five Points of Calvinism," through the exposition of Scripture. In this, my aim is not to exhaust the biblical data or to engage in heavy biblical polemics with differing theological views. Instead, I seek to exposit definitive passages as they pertain to the respective doctrines. My approach is to present and explain the doctrines as plainly as possible by drawing out both the clear teaching of the Bible's text and the necessary implications thereof. The second purpose is one that I find often neglected in treatments of distinctive Reformed doctrines, though to my mind it is equally important.

This purpose is to help believers feel the power of these precious truths in their lives. In other words, I aim not merely to teach the doctrines of grace, but to show what is so great about them. And how great they are! If we really believe the Bible's teaching on the sovereign, mighty, and effectual grace of God, these doctrines not only will be dearly beloved, they will exercise a radical influence on our entire attitude toward God, ourselves, the present life, and the life to come.

I have written this book with an intended audience of those interested in (or alarmed by!) the Reformed view of salvation. There are other books that provide more detailed and extensive treatment of the doctrines of grace, and I would recommend them for the reader's study. But the aim of this book is to present these gracious truths briefly and directly, fortified only by the persuasive power of the plain truth of God's Word. My hope is that Reformed believers will find this book to be a helpful resource to place in the hands of inquiring friends, and that those who already believe the doctrines of grace will drink more deeply of their saving significance. At the heart of my desire, and my prayer to God in offering this book, is that Christians will come to see the grace of God as so great that it transforms their entire spiritual experience. What's so great about the doctrines of grace? It is a fair and important question. May God bless to the readers of this book the Bible's answers, and may God cause more and more of His people to receive the grace revealed in these doctrines to the praise of His wonderful name.

I am grateful to the session and congregation of First Presbyterian Church, Margate, Fla., to which these messages originally were preached, as well as to my present church, Second Presbyterian Church of Greenville, S.C., for their support of my teaching and writing ministry. This book is dedicated to Chuck and Irene Elliott for the gracious spirit of their lives and for their loving devotion to my ministry. Moreover, I thank my beloved wife, Sharon, for the joy and beauty she brings to my life and to our church, as well as our five children for the many sacrifices they cheerfully make because of God's calling on Daddy's life. Lastly, I give praise and glory to the God and Father of my Lord Jesus Christ, with grateful thanks for the transforming power of His grace in my life.

—Richard D. Phillips
Greenville, South Carolina
December 2007

WHAT'S SO GREAT ABOUT THE SOVEREIGNTY OF GOD?

ISAIAH 6:1–7:14

✢ ✢ ✢

In the year that King Uzziah died I saw the Lord sitting upon a throne, high and lifted up; and the train of his robe filled the temple. (Isa. 6:1)

THERE ARE MOMENTS IN LIFE YOU NEVER FORGET: the first time you kiss your spouse, the birth of your first child, your favorite baseball team finally winning the World Series. For many of us, the awakening of our minds to the sovereignty of God is one of these unforgettable moments. "It's like being born again, again," many Christians remark after their faith is renewed by an understanding of the doctrines of grace. Everything changes. It is not that they begin to trust God—all believers must trust God—but that they see the truth about the God they trust. And the truth, as Jesus promised, sets us free: free to rejoice in the glory of a divine grace that truly is gracious.

This book is about the doctrines of grace, biblical teaching about the sovereignty of God at work in our salvation. The doctrines of grace offer a perspective on salvation in which God truly is God, so that everything depends on His will and works to His glory. As with all God's attributes, sovereignty is not a mere abstraction, but a reality that shapes the warp and woof of our experience. The real God is a God who really is sovereign over all reality. Reality in this world is always governed by the statement that begins the Bible: "In the beginning, God . . ." For, in truth, everything—every event, every truth, every experience—begins with God. And so it must be if God really is the God of the Bible: a God who sees all, who knows all, and who is almighty. This is the great truth that opens our eyes to the glory of our sovereign God: He is Alpha and Omega, the beginning and the end of all things. "For from him and through him and to him are all things," Paul writes. "To him be glory forever. Amen" (Rom. 11:36).

By *sovereignty*, we mean that God actively governs everything. By *everything*, we mean all things that happen, from the greatest to the least of occurrences. "Are not two sparrows sold for a penny?" asked Jesus. "Yet not one of them will fall to the ground apart from the will of your Father" (Matt. 10:29, NIV). So *sovereignty* means "according to God's sovereign will." God's sovereignty in salvation means that believers are saved for this sole ultimate reason: "according to God's sovereign will." Or as Paul wrote, our salvation was "predestined according to the purpose of him who works all things according to the counsel of his will" (Eph. 1:11). That sums it up about as well as possible: we are saved according to God's sovereign purpose, by God's sovereign working, according to God's sovereign will. Salvation truly is "from him and through him and to him" (Rom. 11:36). When this truth breaks into our minds and hearts, we glory in God forever.

Isaiah's Vision of Sovereignty

A great many Christians can bear testimony to the earth-shaking effects of realizing the sovereignty of God. These same kinds of testimonies are found in the Bible, perhaps none more profound than the prophet Isaiah's account of his life-changing encounter with the sovereign Lord. If the apostle Paul is the New Testament figure most associated with the teaching of God's sovereignty, his Old Testament counterpart is surely Isaiah. How did Isaiah gain his understanding of God's sovereignty, and what influence did this have on his life? In other words, how would Isaiah answer the question, "What's so great about the sovereignty of God?"

The prophecy of Isaiah contains some of the boldest proclamations of God's sovereignty in Scripture. In chapter 45, he compares God's relationship with mankind to that of a potter and his clay, making of His creation whatever He will. In chapter 46, Isaiah points out the utter sovereignty of God's will: "For I am God, and there is no other; I am God, and there is none like me, declaring the end from the beginning and from ancient times things not yet done, saying, 'My counsel shall stand, and I will accomplish all my purpose'" (Isa. 46:9–10). In chapter 59, Isaiah speaks of God's sovereignty in terms of the long arm of the Lord, by which He is able to will the salvation of His people anywhere: "His own arm brought him salvation, and his righteousness upheld him" (Isa. 59:16).

Isaiah's message about divine sovereignty wouldn't have been any more popular in his time than it is in many circles today. But where did Isaiah get this radical conception of God? Was Isaiah under the influence of eighteenth-century Enlightenment thinking (as is often said of those who espouse his teaching today)? Was Isaiah a closet rationalist, under the influence of Plato and Aristotle, so that he can be written off as a prophet of the Greek philosophers rather than of Israel's God? These can hardly be the case, given that Isaiah wrote in the late eighth and early seventh centuries BC. So where did Isaiah gain these peculiar views in which God is truly God?

The answer is that Isaiah learned of God's sovereignty through his personal experience of the Lord. And he wasn't the only one. Paul got his view of a sovereign Christ on the Damascus Road, Jonah attained his "Calvinism" in the belly of the whale, and Habakkuk gained his grasp of God's sovereignty in his watchtower. In other words, Isaiah—like the other prophets and the apostles, who worshiped God's sovereign glory—gained his doctrine from the Lord Himself.

Isaiah's grasping of God's sovereignty was the great event that changed his life forever. "It was like being born again, again," he might have said about the event that convinced him of sovereign grace. Just like believers today who find that the doctrines of grace change their lives forever, Isaiah's encounter with the sovereign God shaped his life and ministry from that time onward. It was the turning point of his life.

If we can pinpoint the turning point of someone's life, we gain a portal into the very vitals of his or her heart. For one it is the death of a parent. For another it is, sadly, his father walking out on his mother. For still another it is the experience, at long last, of putting on the uniform worn by his father and his father's father before him. Isaiah 6 records the pivotal moment in Isaiah's life, when he gained the insights that governed all the years of his prophetic ministry to come.

Isaiah's turning point was also his call to ministry as a prophet. It came "in the year that King Uzziah died" (Isa. 6:1). Uzziah was one of Judah's great kings. He reigned for fifty-two years of prosperity and expansion. For those of us younger than 52, that would be like having one president govern for our entire lives with a godliness and ability that few modern politicians ever display. With Uzziah as king, Isaiah grew up in a rare period when Judah had been restored to something like the righteousness and prosperity known during the time of David and Solomon.

But now the king was dead, the nation was in mourning, and an unproven youth was taking the throne. Isaiah understandably found himself walking to the temple, seeking consolation. He was from a priestly family, so the temple was a comfortable and familiar place. But this time Isaiah entered the temple to see something wholly unfamiliar. R. C. Sproul, in his singular study of this passage, writes: "The king was dead. But when Isaiah entered the temple he saw another king, the Ultimate

King, the One who sat forever on the throne of Judah. He saw the Lord."[1]

Isaiah tells us what he saw with these words:

> *In the year that King Uzziah died I saw the Lord sitting upon a throne, high and lifted up; and the train of his robe filled the temple. Above him stood the seraphim. Each had six wings: with two he covered his face, and with two he covered his feet, and with two he flew. And one called to another and said: "Holy, holy, holy is the LORD of hosts; the whole earth is full of his glory!" And the foundations of the thresholds shook at the voice of him who called, and the house was filled with smoke. (Isa. 6:1–4)*

Uzziah's death had brought a crisis of sovereignty. In that crisis, Isaiah's eyes were opened to behold the true Sovereign in Israel, the true King who sat enthroned over the nation. His vision revealed *the sovereignty of God.* There was the Lord Himself, "high and lifted up." Uzziah had gone down to the grave, vacating his throne in Jerusalem, but Yahweh reigned on high. Isaiah saw Him seated, firmly ensconced in the place of regal authority.

Notice the details that Isaiah provides, all of which speak to God's utter sovereignty. He says that "the train of his robe filled the temple." As God sat enthroned, His regal garments filled the temple, His throne room, leaving no room for another. God utterly fills the sphere of sovereignty. Isaiah would express this truth over and over by saying on God's behalf: "I am God, and there is no other" (Isa. 46:9). Not only is God sovereign, He *alone* is sovereign. "My glory I give to no other" (Isa. 42:8), He insists.

How easily we bring things into our lives alongside the presence of God. How often we consider our allegiance to God as just one of many commitments, the Lord as one of many we seek to please. But He does not accept a shared sovereignty.

Isaiah saw other beings in this throne room. He relates: "Above him stood the seraphim. Each had six wings: with two he covered his face, and with two he covered his feet, and with two he flew" (Isa. 6:2). These angels were standing in deference while the Lord was seated. Though they are beings of great glory, they covered their faces in awe of God. They covered their feet in creaturely humility, just as Moses had to remove his sandals before the burning bush. They also were flying, indicating their readiness to perform God's will without hesitation. Awe, humility, readiness to serve—this is the angels' example of how the sovereign God is to be worshiped.

The angels were calling to one another: "Holy, holy, holy is the LORD of hosts; the whole earth is full of his glory!" (Isa. 6:3). Here we have an insight about the worship of heaven. It is God-centered, focused on the glory of God's attributes, especially His thrice-exalted holiness. Holiness is the sum of who and what God is. His is a holy love, a holy goodness, a holy wrath, and a holy faithfulness. Holiness is God's exalted singularity, the separation between God and His creatures, between the holy God and all evil. If the holy angels must cover their faces for the glory of God, how much more should men fall prostrate as sinners before so holy a Lord!

Finally, the prophet tells us what he felt and smelled: "And the foundations of the thresholds shook at the voice of him who called, and the house was filled with smoke" (Isa. 6:4). By now we surely get the idea: this God is not to be toyed with, manipulated, or offended. How much less did Isaiah find that heavenly assembly boring or irrelevant, as so many people today say of theology. Indeed, the effect on Isaiah was shattering: "And I said: 'Woe is me! For I am lost; for I am a man of unclean lips, and I dwell in the midst of a people of unclean lips; for my eyes have seen the King, the LORD of hosts!'" (Isa. 6:5).

"Woe!" Isaiah pronounces—the first of many prophetic "woes" he would utter over the years—and he cries it against himself. Isaiah despaired of himself and all his works. You know you have met with God when you cry, "Woe is me!" This is what self-awareness produces when accompanied by God-awareness. Here we see the link between the sovereignty of God's grace and the self-abandonment that flows from the doctrine of total depravity. These truths go together, like two parts of a locket. When these pieces click, the good news of God's grace in Jesus Christ makes sense as it never has before.

Isaiah's gospel also was centered on a savingly effective atonement. A generation such as ours that finds it hard to accept God's sovereignty also finds it increasingly hard to accept the atonement of Christ. But apart from an atonement for sin, a meeting with the thrice-holy God can only be disastrous for depraved men. This is why the Bible's gospel of salvation centers on the atoning work of Christ. And what happened next to Isaiah was all about the atonement of Christ: "Then one of the seraphim flew to me, having in his hand a burning coal that he had taken with tongs from the altar. And he touched my mouth and said: 'Behold, this has touched your lips; your guilt is taken away, and your sin atoned for'" (Isa. 6:6–7). Atoning grace was applied to the place where Isaiah most keenly felt his sin—his lips—sanctifying the instrument by which he would serve God as a prophet. So it must be for us all: true service to God flows from the application of Christ's redeeming work to our lives.

In Isaiah's life and ministry, we see perhaps more clearly than anywhere else in the Bible the impact of an awareness of the sovereignty of God. What's so great about the sovereignty of God? What difference does God's sovereignty make? For Isaiah, it meant everything. In his response to the vision of God's sovereign lordship, we can observe four hallmarks that will also play out in our experience as our faith is centered on a biblical vision of the sovereign grace of God.

A Readiness to Serve

I have been saying that everything in a believer's life changes when he or she grasps the truth of God's sovereignty. The first change for Isaiah came immediately upon his vision of the Lord enthroned. The first mark of his awareness of God's utter sovereignty was a readiness to serve: "And I heard the voice of the Lord saying, 'Whom shall I send, and who will go for us?' Then I said, 'Here am I! Send me'" (Isa. 6:8). We don't know about Isaiah's attitude prior to receiving this vision, but we do know what it was immediately afterward. Seeing God's sovereign glory, he exclaimed, "Here am I! Send me."

Since God is the true sovereign, there is no greater privilege than to serve Him. Awe before His glory makes other pursuits diminish. Not all are called to the prophetic office. God calls people to be carpenters, lawyers, doctors, sound engineers, and garbage men. But those who have seen the sovereignty of God see all of their labor as an opportunity to extend His reign and serve His kingdom. It is when we realize how great is the God we serve, how total is His sovereignty over all, and how glorious is His kingdom that we want to serve Him in all we do. Isaiah had not even learned what labor God had in mind for him, but when he heard the question, "Whom shall I send?" his newly consecrated lips broke forth: "Here am I! Send me." If we see just a portion of what he saw, we will do the same, considering not the difficulties but the high privilege of serving so great a Lord.

Many people do not believe in God's sovereignty, yet still serve the Lord. But there is a great difference. Those who see the Lord in His sovereign glory have an inward compulsion to serve this God. Serving God is the glory of their lives. Their service is measured not so much in what they achieve—or what God achieves through them—but rather in the sheer wonder of the God they serve. Like little boys dividing up into teams on the playground, being picked to play on this team is the greatest joy imaginable, especially for those who are so unworthy. "Here am I! Send me," is not merely the response of those who see God's sovereign glory, it is their delight. Since God is certain to be glorified, they want to be among those glorifying God.

Humble, Trusting Obedience

A second mark of an awareness of God's sovereignty appears in this passage: a humble, trusting obedience to God's commands. Chapter 6 concludes with God's description of what He wanted Isaiah to do, the shock of which caused even the awe-struck prophet to flinch:

> *And he said, "Go, and say to this people: 'Keep on hearing, but do not understand; keep on seeing, but do not perceive.' Make the heart of this people dull, and their ears heavy, and blind their eyes; lest they see with their eyes, and hear with their ears, and understand with their hearts, and turn and be healed." Then I said, "How long, O Lord?" (Isa. 6:9–11)*

Isaiah's calling was to bring about a hardening in Jerusalem. His ministry would cause calluses as a prelude to judgment, because God intended first to purify and only then to deliver His people. We can hear Isaiah stifle a cry at this instruction, yet without complaint, without quarreling with the wisdom of his Sovereign. He simply asked the reasonable question, "How long, O Lord?" The answer could not have failed to shock the prophet:

And he said: "Until cities lie waste without inhabitant, and houses without people, and the land is a desolate waste, and the Lord removes people far away, and the forsaken places are many in the midst of the land. And though a tenth remain in it, it will be burned again, like a terebinth or an oak, whose stump remains when it is felled." The holy seed is its stump. (Isa. 6:11–13)

Undoubtedly, Isaiah entered the temple because he was concerned for the well-being of Jerusalem with King Uzziah gone. Having met the true Sovereign, he learned of terrors far beyond his original fears. But Isaiah is singular among the major prophets in that he never complained. He had seen a sovereign, saving God. If he was called to a ministry of hardening, then hardening it would be. It did not occur to Isaiah that he knew better than the Lord of Hosts. If it pleased the Lord through a faithful ministry to reduce His church to the stump of a holy seed, then Isaiah would make that remnant the object of his labor.

A similar commitment to God's saving sovereignty would inspire us to a humble, trusting obedience to God's Word. Relying on God's sovereign purpose, knowing that there is a decree of marvelous grace behind everything that happens, we can face difficult circumstances without wavering from God's law. We can face the hostility of the world or even the apostasy of the church without faltering in our ministry. We can trust the wisdom and obey the commands of a sovereign God who works all things out according to the purpose of His holy will.

As Isaiah later declared: "I will wait for the LORD, who is hiding his face from the house of Jacob. I will put my trust in him" (Isa. 8:17, NIV).

Holy Boldness

A third mark of Isaiah's ministry surfaces in the passage that immediately follows, a passage that is surely linked in theme to chapter 6 even if the events are separated by almost a decade. Jotham, Uzziah's son and successor, had finished his reign. It had been a time of decline and the beginning of decay. But with Jotham's successor, Ahaz, a period of flagrant disobedience to God was about to begin.

The proximate cause of the trouble was an invasion of Judah by the northern nation of Israel along with its neighbor Aram. Unbelieving Ahaz began hunting around for a worldly ally who would bail him out, even if it meant leading his people into idolatry. His choice was Assyria, the growing power on the northern side of his enemies. But God sent Isaiah to confront and proclaim a message to this king:

> Say to him, "Be careful, be quiet, do not fear, and do not let your heart be faint because of these two smoldering stumps of firebrands, at the fierce anger of Rezin and Syria and the son of Remaliah. Because Syria, with Ephraim and the son of Remaliah, has devised evil against you, saying, 'Let us go up against Judah and terrify it, and let us conquer it for ourselves, and set up the son of Tabeel as king in the midst of

*it,' thus says the Lord GOD: 'It shall not stand, and it shall
not come to pass.'" (Isa. 7:4–7)*

God's message to Ahaz was an application of the vision Isaiah
had seen earlier: the mighty kings of Israel and Aram were not
real sovereigns. The true Sovereign is the Lord who reigns over
all. Isaiah pointed this out to King Ahaz with classic words calling
for faith: "If you are not firm in faith, you will not be firm at all"
(Isa. 7:9).

This was the message God sent Isaiah to deliver to King Ahaz,
a monarch equipped with all his earthly sovereignty. If you don't
think this was a frightening encounter, you are kidding yourself.
Most of us are terrified at the thought of mentioning God to
friends at work, much less issuing an ultimatum to a king. But
that is the difference it makes to have seen the sovereignty of
God. Whatever fear Isaiah felt for King Ahaz was brushed aside
by his much greater fear of the sovereign Lord God.

A consciousness of God's sovereignty bestows in us *a holy
boldness* before the world and its powers. This is what made
Isaiah useful: he could proclaim the Word of the Lord, even
the word of judgment, to a decadent and dangerous generation. "Ah, sinful nation," he accused in the opening chapter, "a
people laden with iniquity, offspring of evildoers, children who
deal corruptly! They have forsaken the LORD, they have despised
the Holy One of Israel, they are utterly estranged" (Isa. 1:4). I
realize that this kind of talk may not fill a stadium today. It may
not place a congregation on the roster of church-growth success
stories. But the willingness to speak the truth of God, preaching

God's judgment to a generation as depraved as ours, is a sure sign that the speaker has beheld the sovereignty of God.

The great Scottish Reformer, John Knox, was another prophetic figure who was famous for his brave confrontations with the Catholic Mary, Queen of Scots. Once Knox was asked how he could defy the queen's religious views so audaciously, given that she was the sovereign of the land. Knox famously replied, "When you have just spent time on your knees before the King of Kings, you do not find the Queen of Scotland to be so frightening." Awareness of the sovereignty of God, especially as it brings us to our knees in supplication before His throne of grace, gives us the holy boldness so desperately needed in our time.

Reliance on Sovereign, Saving Grace

Finally, we see in the prophet Isaiah a sure mark that he had beheld the Lord in His sovereign majesty—an utter reliance on God's sovereign, saving grace.

This is seen in the sign Isaiah gave to King Ahaz. Isaiah urged this sign on Ahaz to enliven his faith. It was a sign that was foolish in the eyes of the world, but glorious in the eyes of God: "Behold, the virgin shall conceive and bear a son, and shall call his name Immanuel" (Isa. 7:14). In the presence of Ahaz's apostate unbelief, Isaiah laid his hand on the greatest sign of sovereign grace of which he could think: the virgin who would be with child.

Later, Isaiah would speak of childbirth through a barren womb as a sign of saving grace (Isa. 54:1). A barren womb represents human labor that has failed. But the virgin womb speaks of a field where man has not sown at all. From that womb comes the Savior, Jesus Christ. Imagine how little a man such as Ahaz would have esteemed the birth of a baby as a reason to trust God with his problems, just as many today consider the preaching of the gospel to be "foolishness." But both the divinely incarnated baby and the preaching of His gospel today are the power of God for the salvation of those who believe.

This reminds us that a true gospel ministry can succeed only if a virgin girl gives birth to a son. What foolishness to the world! But she has. And the miracle of grace continues today. If this does not encourage us to labor in the otherwise barren fields of prayer and simple Bible preaching, not to mention humility, long-suffering, self-denial, and holy obedience to God, then nothing ever will. Isaiah's sign of the virgin birth tells us not to trust human wisdom, even as we must not despair in the face of human difficulty or personal failure. For if we, like Isaiah, gain a vision of God's sovereign glory, especially in the salvation of sinners, we will count it our privilege to serve this sovereign Lord, who brought our Savior into the world through a virgin womb, and who will bring many to salvation as we likewise rely on His sovereign, saving grace.

2

WHAT'S SO GREAT ABOUT TOTAL DEPRAVITY?

ROMANS 3:10—18

✣ ✣ ✣

As it is written: "None is righteous, no, not one; no one understands; no one seeks for God. All have turned aside; together they have become worthless; no one does good, not even one." (Rom. 3:10–12)

MALCOLM MUGGERIDGE, THE FAMOUS British journalist, had a life-changing experience that was very different from that of the prophet Isaiah. Yet in one important respect it was quite similar: they both came to a piercing awareness of their depraved spiritual condition. But whereas Isaiah learned to say "Woe is me!" in the face of God, Muggeridge learned it in the face of a leper woman.

On assignment in India, Muggeridge went to a river for a swim. As he entered the water, his eyes fell on a woman bathing. He felt an impulse to go to her and seduce her, just as King David felt when he saw Bathsheba. Temptation storming his mind, he began swimming toward her. The words of his wedding vows came to his mind, but he responded by just going faster. The voice of allurement called out, "Stolen water is sweet" (Prov. 9:17), and he swam more furiously still. But when he pulled up near the woman and she turned, Muggeridge saw, "She was a leper. . . . This creature grinned at me, showing a toothless mask." His first reaction was to despise her: "What a dirty lecherous woman!" he thought. But then it crashed in on him that it was not the woman who was lecherous; it was his own heart.[2] This is precisely the teaching of the Bible about the moral and spiritual condition of men and women: our hearts are corrupt, our minds are depraved, and our desires are enslaved to the passions of sin.

It was not by chance that Isaiah felt his depravity when confronted with God's holy presence, any more than it was by chance that Muggeridge's glimpse of his true condition led to his conversion to Christianity. One way to put this is that theology and anthropology are always linked. In order to understand the truth about yourself and other people, you have to see the truth about God—and vice versa. John Calvin made this point in his *Institutes of the Christian Religion*, commenting that one may begin a study of theology either with God or with man, since to know either correctly you must correctly know the other.

What We Really Need to Know about Us

This insight is reflected in the order of topics covered by the doctrines of grace. Not only are the doctrines lined up to form an acronym based on the Dutch flower "TULIP," there is a sound theological logic to the ordering. In particular, it is significant that total depravity comes first. Perhaps more so than even our beliefs about God, our doctrine of man is at stake in the doctrines of grace. Indeed, I would argue that while most of the attention is devoted to the second letter of the acronym—U, for unconditional election—the true controversy resides in the first letter—T, for total depravity. In short, the central controversy regarding the doctrines of grace may be summed up in this question: "I'm not *totally* depraved, am I?"

It is understandable that we want to know the truth about ourselves. The issues that really matter are not the trivial facts of our lives but the essential truths of our nature and standing before God. In this respect, I am reminded of a picture that is printed in one of the best-selling church-growth books of recent years. The picture is labeled "Our Target," and the man featured in it is designated "Saddleback Sam," so named for the author's church. Around the picture are things the author thinks are important for us to know about the target audience of our ministry. Included are such insights as "he is well-educated," "he likes contemporary music," "health and fitness are high priorities for him," and "he prefers the casual and informal over the formal." From this sociological perspective on people arises a sociological approach to ministry and, ultimately, to salvation.

The apostle Paul also wanted us to know important truths about ourselves, though his interests were somewhat different from the above. His portrait of mankind is found in Romans 3:10–18. Assembling his portrait not from consumer surveys but from the Old Testament, Paul tells us about our moral and spiritual condition. It is not a pretty picture: "None is righteous, no, not one; no one understands; no one seeks for God. . . . There is no fear of God before their eyes." From such a biblical consideration of mankind arises a biblical and theological approach to ministry and salvation.

It is the distinction of adherents to Reformed theology in general and to the doctrines of grace in particular that, following the Scriptures, we hold to the worst possible view of man—and therefore, we exercise the highest possible reliance on God's grace. If the question is "How bad am I really?" we answer, "Much, much worse than you have dared to think." It is against the backdrop of this terrible news about man in sin that we see the good news of the gospel as something far more wonderful than we have ever imagined.

The Doctrine of Total Depravity

The question of man's depravity considers not the extent of his guilt before God, but the extent of his corruption in sin. The question is: am I totally depraved or only partly depraved? This is not to say there is nothing good about us. In fact, we need to emphasize that humankind was created good, bearing the image of God. The most depraved person you will ever meet enjoys the dignity of God's original glorious creation of mankind. The doctrine of total depravity does not teach that men and women are "worthless"; as Francis Schaeffer passionately argued, "Though the Bible says men are lost, it does not say they are nothing."[3] Far from it: it is the priceless value of every human soul that defines the tragedy expressed by total depravity. Neither does total depravity mean that little children should never be called "good boy" or "good girl." It is very possible for totally depraved sinners to do things that are in and of themselves good.

So what is total depravity really about? Loraine Boettner explains:

> This doctrine of Total Inability, which declares that men are dead in sin, does not mean that all men are equally bad, nor that any man is as bad as he could be, nor that anyone is entirely destitute of virtue, nor that human will is evil in itself, nor that man's spirit is inactive, and much less does it mean that the body is dead. What it does mean is that since the fall man rests under the curse of sin, that he is actuated by wrong principles, and that he is wholly unable to love God or to do anything meriting salvation.[4]

Given this definition, some people refer to this doctrine as *radical* depravity, which may better express the point. Arthur Pink explains: "The entrance of sin into the human constitution has affected every part and faculty of man's being. . . . Man is unable to realize his own aspirations and materialize his own ideals. He cannot do the things that he would. There is a moral inability which paralyzes him."[5]

Paul expresses this truth in classically biblical language, and in Romans 3:10–18 we can see the truth that man is radically depraved and how this depravity works out in our experience.

Unrighteousness

First, Paul makes the summary pronouncement that "none is righteous, no, not one" (Rom. 3:10). *Righteousness* is a legal term; it denotes our standing before God's justice. Paul's earlier teaching in Romans makes it clear that righteousness before God comes through the law. Romans 2:13 states, "It is not the hearers of the law who are righteous before God, but the doers of the law who will be justified." If these are the terms, then we must begin our understanding of salvation by recognizing that everybody needs it. People have all kinds of needs: companionship, employment, and even training in life skills. But a far more profound need stands behind all these, and it is for this need that the gospel is preached—our need to gain righteousness before God. Unless we are justified before God, the wrath of God abides on us.

If perfect obedience to the law of God is the divine standard of righteousness—and it is—then there is not a single person who does not need to be justified before God. And if a single sin is sufficient to condemn us to eternal punishment, as the Bible says it is (see James 2:10), then everyone who has committed sin needs to be justified above all else. And if Solomon was right when he said that "there is no one who does not sin" (1 Kings 8:46)—and our universal experience confirms that he was right—then God sent His Son to the cross to provide the solution to the greatest need of every person.

As if our experience does not prove this well enough, Paul elaborates on the condition of fallen man that has contributed to his claim that "None is righteous, no, not one." This is the greatest problem of every sinner. Francis Schaeffer envisions a conversation that proceeds this way: "Why do I need salvation?" "Because you are under the wrath of God." "And just why am I under the wrath of God?" The answer to that crucial question is man's total depravity, as worked out by Paul in the verses that follow Romans 3:10.[6] This depravity begins in our manner of thinking. The centrality of the mind is frequently emphasized by Paul, as by other biblical writers. Having stated man's unrighteousness, he begins to trace man's depravity by writing, "No one understands" (Rom. 3:11).

A Depraved Mind

There are few things worse than living a lie, yet this is the universal human experience. Sin has corrupted man's thinking in such a way that people lack the ability to understand the truth about themselves, God, and the world. This is why Jesus told Nicodemus, "Unless one is born again he cannot see the kingdom of God" (John 3:3). Until we are saved out of our depraved state, we are blind to the reality of God's glory and righteousness.

Reflecting on Paul's teaching that "no one understands," Reformed theologians speak of fallen man's *spiritual inability*. Imagine owning a broken radio that lacks the ability to receive signals on certain frequencies. The signals are being sent, but you are unable to receive them. This is man's condition when it comes to God. Elsewhere, Paul states this clearly: "The natural person does not accept the things of the Spirit of God, for they are folly to him, and he is not able to understand them because they are spiritually discerned" (1 Cor. 2:14). The key statement here is not merely that man in sin *does not* accept the truth of God, but that man in sin *is not able* to receive the things of God.

Jesus taught this no less forcefully than Paul. Explaining the Pharisees' persistent unbelief, He said: "Why do you not understand what I say? It is because you cannot bear to hear my word" (John 8:43). This makes an important distinction, because Jesus explained that man's unbelief is not a result of the Bible's obscurity. The reason "no one understands" does not reside in a lack of clarity of God's revealed Word. Jesus explained that His teaching was misunderstood because His message was intolerable to sinful hearts. At the heart of sinful mankind's total depravity is his moral and spiritual inability to accept the gospel.

Being rooted in spiritual ignorance, man's total depravity manifests itself in idolatry. Paul's catalog of depravity continues, "No one seeks for God" (Rom. 3:11). In his quest for meaning, truth, and salvation, fallen mankind will turn everywhere except to God. This is why such manifestly foolish ideas as the theory of evolution gain so much traction in our world, propping up fallen man's desperate quest to find a replacement for God. As Calvin famously quipped, "Man's nature, so to speak, is a perpetual factory of idols."[7] This being the case, the one thing depraved man will not do is seek after God.

This does not mean that people do not desire the blessings of God, for they most certainly do. Man is seeking peace, prosperity, and joy. This is why unbelievers are often happy to come to church, so long as the preacher sticks to "life-skills" topics, agreeing never to mention essential biblical themes such as sin, atonement, and justification. Depraved man is always glad for God's gifts, so long as he doesn't have to deal with God Himself. Yet how unsatisfying is such a life. Perhaps the greatest tragedy of today's hyper-affluent yet terminally unsatisfied Western society is that the only One capable of satisfying our souls is also the One whom depraved sinners will not seek. "No one seeks for God," Paul says, delivering a death blow to every scheme of conversion that relies on man's initiative in accepting the gospel.

Moral and Spiritual Bondage

Fallen man is unrighteous. Fallen man sins against God just as surely as "fish got to swim, birds got to fly," because, first, he is spiritually unable to receive God's truth, and, second, as a born idolater, he will not seek for God. Third, Paul tells us that fallen man is enslaved to sin. Paul says, "All have turned aside; together they have become worthless; no one does good, not even one" (Rom. 3:12).

Even a cursory inventory of our spiritual anatomy proves
that this is true. Paul starts with our speech: "'Their throat is an
open grave; they use their tongues to deceive.' 'The venom of
asps is under their lips.' 'Their mouth is full of curses and bitterness'" (Rom. 3:13–14, quoting Pss. 5:9; 140:3; 10:7). Tak-ing
these citations from the Old Testament, Paul points out the filth
and venom that spew from human mouths. He is not talking
about merely a few potty mouths! These comments could be
said of you and of me; they describe well the kinds of things we
have said to and about others. Our speech reeks of the grave. We
are such masters of deception and falsity that Christians who
have learned to speak the truth in love have entered a high realm
of sanctification. Like the sacs of venom behind the fangs of a
snake, so is our speech. It is filled with "curses and bitterness."

In the first seminary class I ever attended, we were given a
humbling assignment. We were told to go an entire week without sinning with our tongues, and then to write a paper about it.
I did not last the afternoon, and every student's paper spoke of
wretched failure. And these students were all Christians in training for pastoral ministry! Our depravity pours out of our mouths
like sewage from a pipe.

Paul proceeds to our "ways": "Their feet are swift to shed
blood; in their paths are ruin and misery, and the way of peace
they have not known" (Rom. 3:15–17). Man is violent, as the
newspaper testifies every day. Unable to live in harmony, we
easily develop anger and malice toward others. If we can get
away with it, we respond with violence. A couple in my church
reported their experience at a marriage seminar. A thousand

Christian couples sat tensely at their tables as it began. The conference leader began by asking each of them to look across the table into the eyes of the man or woman he or she had fallen in love with and married, and then to say, "You are not my enemy." The couple told me, "You could have cut the air with a knife" as husbands and wives struggled to face the reality of their marital hostility.

Lastly, Paul sums up our depravity: "There is no fear of God before their eyes" (Rom. 3:18). Man is at enmity with God in every possible arena. Man wants to dethrone God and place himself in God's seat—mimicking the sinful heart of the great deceiver, Satan. D. Martyn Lloyd-Jones writes: "They hate God. They are against him and all his laws. It is because they are dominated by the devil, the hater of God, who is reproducing himself in them."[8]

Reformed Christians speak in terms of *the bondage of the will*, a doctrine closely allied to total depravity. Man insists that his will is free, when in fact he is a slave to sin and the Devil. It's not that our choices aren't real—they are. But because of our total depravity, we lack the power to will after God. The bondage is within us. With sin corrupting our every faculty, we are no more able to will after God than a blind man can see, a deaf man can hear, or a mute man can speak.

This is the terrible, dark secret about sin. Sin promises freedom but delivers slavery. Some Jews once objected to Jesus' teaching of this fact, saying, "We . . . have never been enslaved to anyone" (John 8:33). Jesus replied in scathing terms: "Truly, truly, I say to you, everyone who commits sin is a slave to sin"

(John 8:34). His explanation was even more severe: "You are of your father the devil, and your will is to do your father's desires" (John 8:44). This is the state of man's will after the fall: enslaved to the desire of the Devil. Man's bondage in sin results not from the lack of opportunity to do good and love God, but from the bondage of his heart that causes him to love evil and hate God. Here is the rub when it comes to total depravity: despite the glorious opportunity afforded to man in the gospel of Jesus Christ, such is our total depravity that we are *not able* in and of ourselves to turn to God.

What's So Great about Total Depravity?

"I'm not *totally* depraved, am I?" people object. The answer from the Bible, and the testimony of universal human experience, is, "Yes, you really are." But even if we have to accept that this is, in fact, the Bible's teaching, it's not obvious why we should like it. This is why some find it odd that Calvinists seem to love total depravity (the doctrine, not the condition) so much. Their question is, "What's so great about the doctrine of total depravity?"

I would offer three answers to this important question. For the doctrine of total depravity is not just something we learn so as to score high marks on some theology exam. Instead, total depravity is a doctrine to live by.

The first answer is that through the lens of a biblical understanding of ourselves, *we come to appreciate the gospel truly.* The only way to see the greatness of the gospel is to see how bad is our plight. Or to put it differently, unless we know what we are being saved from, we really don't grasp the glory of our salvation.

People say the doctrines of grace are boring and irrelevant, and that we need to preach something else to keep their attention in church. But this could be said only by someone who *does not* sense the depth of his problem before God. Indeed, it is when we best see our lost condition that we most treasure the gospel. This is what the doctrine of total depravity tells us—that the only way someone like this, someone like you and me, is going to be made right with God is by radical grace. And when we combine an accurate appraisal of man's total depravity with a biblical vision of the absolute holiness of God, we see the gospel in all its glory. It is when we set God's high and right demands next to our low and base performance, and when we compare His glorious being with our utter corruption, that we see the true problem of life. This is the great gulf between us and God, indeed an infinite one, as high as the heavens are above the earth. It is a problem that could be solved, a chasm that could be spanned, only on a hill far away, on an old rugged cross, "where the dearest and best for a world of lost sinners was slain."[9]

The second answer is that the doctrine of total depravity is *vital to all true spirituality*. At least this is what Isaiah 57:15 tells us: "For thus says the One who is high and lifted up, who inhabits eternity, whose name is Holy: 'I dwell in the high and holy place, and also with him who is of a contrite and lowly spirit, to revive the spirit of the lowly, and to revive the heart of the contrite.'" Do you want the high and holy God to dwell in your heart? Then humble yourself before Him with the truth about yourself, and look in total reliance to His grace for your salvation.

This is what marked the difference between the Pharisee and the tax collector of whom Jesus spoke in Luke 18. The two men went into the temple to pray. The one thanked God for how good he had become, though admittedly with some help from the Lord. The other refused even to look upward, but beat his breast and cried out, "God be merciful to me, a sinner!" (Luke 18:13). Jesus commented, "I tell you, this man went down to his house justified, rather than the other. For everyone who exalts himself will be humbled, but the one who humbles himself will be exalted" (Luke 18:14).

Likewise, it was when the prodigal son realized what a swine he had become that he finally turned his heart to his father. His return to spiritual life was marked with the words, "I am no longer worthy" (Luke 15:19, 21). This is true spirituality, for it leads us home to God.

The third answer is that total depravity *exalts the cross* in our eyes and fills our hearts with a holy delight. I think about a pastoral encounter I had some time ago. A young man came to speak with me about his lack of spiritual joy. He began by informing me that his doctrine was impeccable. He fully subscribed to all five points of Calvinism. He accepted covenant theology and despised all "inferior" products. But, he went on, "I just don't feel anything." Then he asked, "Is that a problem?"

How do you respond to such a question? I answered that, so far as his testimony was true, he did *not* have impeccable doctrine, nor did he even subscribe to the truths of the doctrines of grace. Not really, anyway. In short, if in his entire Christian life he had never "felt anything," as he insisted was the case, then the reality was that his Christian life had never really existed.

In ministering to this young man, I did not start by expounding the doctrine of election; in such a situation, it would be silly to inquire, "Do you think you are elect?" Neither did I expound on God's marvelous love. The question, "Don't you know that God loves you and has a wonderful plan for your life?" can have no meaning to someone who has heard the gospel but felt nothing. Instead, I started where Paul started in Romans and where the doctrines of grace truly begin. I said, "Evidently, you do not realize what a wretched person you truly are, and what an offense your depravity is in the holy sight of God, if you can feel nothing in response to the atoning death of God's Son."

Without a quickened awareness of our depravity, we are Pharisees at best, though most of us are far worse. The best we can approach is a religious performance that brings glory to us and leaves us looking down on everybody else, just the way many Christians today look down on the rest of society, the Pharisee gazing down on the abortion doctor and the pervert.

Jesus knew Pharisees well, and He didn't like them. Far better to Him was the sinful woman who burst in at the home of a Pharisee named Simon and threw herself at Jesus' feet. Jesus said to him: "Do you see this woman? I entered your house; you gave me no water for my feet, but she has wet my feet with her tears and wiped them with her hair. . . . Therefore I tell you, her sins, which are many, are forgiven—for she loved much. But he who is forgiven little, loves little" (Luke 7:44, 47).

Awe and gratitude drive the true Christian life and draw us joyfully to God's grace in Christ. It is from the pit of our lost condition that we gaze up toward a God so high and perfect in His holiness. But from that vantage point we come to see fully at least one of those four dimensions of the cross that Paul would long to have us know: its height. The cross of Christ then rises up to span the full and vast distance that marks how far short we are of the glory of God, and that cross becomes exceedingly precious in our eyes.

I will give thanks to you, O LORD, for though you were angry with me, your anger turned away, that you might comfort me. Behold, God is my salvation; I will trust, and will not be afraid; for the LORD GOD is my strength and my song, and he has become my salvation. (Isa. 12:1–2)

3

WHAT'S SO GREAT ABOUT UNCONDITIONAL ELECTION?

ROMANS 9:10—24

✢ ✢ ✢

For he says to Moses, "I will have mercy on whom I have mercy, and I will have compassion on whom I have compassion." So then it depends not on human will or exertion, but on God, who has mercy. (Rom. 9:15–16)

MOST PEOPLE ARE KNOWN ACCORDING TO some reputation. Farmers are known for having red necks. When you think of lawyers, you think (rightly or wrongly) of a certain looseness with the truth. Athletes have the reputation of being less than world-class scholars, doctors are thought to have poor bedside manners, and Calvinists are known by our belief in predestination. "You're a Calvinist? Do you really believe that God predetermined every-thing that would ever happen long beforehand?" Such a question has been heard by practically every person who has ever espoused the doctrines of grace.

The doctrine of unconditional election does not, in fact, sum up the entire Reformed faith or even the five points of Calvinism. As I argued in the previous chapter, the doctrine of total depravity is at least as fundamental to Reformed theology and more genuinely controversial. But Calvinism is known for teaching predestination, and on the basis of this doctrine the whole house of sovereign grace largely stands or falls.

Unconditional Election in Romans 9

The doctrine of unconditional election, or predestination, was not invented by John Calvin. Calvin largely reproduced the teachings of the fourth- and fifth-century theologian Augustine. But Augustine did not invent predestination either. He got it from the apostle Paul, who also did not invent predestination, since it is taught all through the Bible, starting in the Old Testament and continuing strongly in the teachings of Jesus. The doctrine of predestination comes from God, for God has revealed it as an important description of the way He interacts with the creation He has made.

When I was teaching college, I was working in my office one day when a student knocked on my door. She introduced herself and immediately said, "Sir, I would like to know if you believe in predestination." The reply I gave her has become something of a stock answer for me. I said: "It doesn't matter what I believe. The question is, 'Does the Bible teach predestination?'" Let's make that our question as well.

In fact, predestination is taught all through the Bible. A famous Old Testament example is Isaiah 46:9–10: "I am God, and there is none like me, declaring the end from the beginning and from ancient times things not yet done, saying, 'My counsel shall stand, and I will accomplish all my purpose.'" The New Testament is chock-full of teachings on predestination, including Paul's frank statement to the Athenians that God created man to "inhabit the whole earth; and he determined the times set for them and the exact places where they should live" (Acts 17:26, NIV). For a clear teaching on predestination in salvation, we have Jesus' statement in John 6:39: "And this is the will of him who sent me, that I should lose nothing of all that he has given me."

Is there a specific chapter of the Bible where the doctrine receives more careful and straightforward treatment? Yes—the ninth chapter of Paul's letter to the Romans. Paul teaches in the previous chapter on the absolute character of God's grace, concluding with the glorious statement that nothing "in all creation, will be able to separate us from the love of God in Christ Jesus our Lord" (Rom. 8:39). But this raises an immediate question: what happened to the Jews? If nothing can separate Christians from God's love, how did the Jews become separated from God's love? This is the context for Paul's teaching in Romans 9 on unconditional election.

Paul answers by first affirming his deep love for the Jews and his anguish over their unbelief (9:1–3). He admits the privileges and glories that are assigned to God's old covenant people (9:4–5). But this does not mean that God somehow failed when it came to Israel, since God never promised or intended that every last Israelite would be saved. The fact that Abraham's son Isaac received the covenant and his older brother Ishmael did not proves this (9:6–9). The reason was that God chose one and not another. Then Paul points out that this is stated explicitly when it comes to the twin brothers Jacob and Esau. Not only did God choose one for salvation and not the other, He revealed this choice to their mother before they were even born. It is at this point that Paul launches into his defense of unconditional election:

> *And not only so, but also when Rebecca had conceived children by one man, our forefather Isaac, though they were not yet born and had done nothing either good or bad—in order that God's purpose of election might continue, not because of works but because of his call—she was told, "The older will serve the younger." As it is written, "Jacob I loved, but Esau I hated." (Rom. 9:10–13)*

In these verses, Paul effectively states the doctrine of predestination, citing the example of Jacob and Esau, one of whom was predestined to inherit the covenant blessings while the other was not. Predestination teaches that God sovereignly ordains in advance that some people will be saved (or receive other covenant blessings) and that others will not. The expression *unconditional election* in the doctrines of grace means that without anything commendable in themselves, some people have been chosen by God to come to Christ and be saved. This "election" or "choosing" took place in eternity past, as Paul states in Ephesians 1:4: God "chose us in [Christ] before the foundation of the world." Long before they were born or had done anything good or bad (Rom. 9:11), the elect were known to God and were chosen by His free and sovereign grace.

Objection # 1: Not Fair!

If you have never heard this taught, it is almost certain that an objection has formed immediately in your mind: "That's not fair! It's not fair for God arbitrarily to choose some people instead of others, without any consideration of merit or deserving!" This is the main objection of Arminian theology, so named for the sixteenth- and seventeenth-century theologian Jacob Arminius, who famously waged this criticism. In the words of a modern Arminian scholar:

> Arminians hold that since the very nature of God is holy love, God unconditionally loves all of his creatures and sincerely acts to promote their true flourishing and well-being. This is why Arminians reject the Reformed doctrine of election as unthinkable, for that doctrine holds that God unconditionally chooses to save some, while passing over the rest, thereby consigning them to eternal misery. A God of unconditional love would never pass over any of his lost creatures in this fashion.[10]

This is a helpful quotation, because it not only articulates the Arminian objection but also exposes numerous errors in thinking about this subject. Essentially, the Arminian denial of unconditional election is based on a rational conviction about what is and what is not possible or appropriate to God. Therefore, the first question we need to ask is this: are Christians to believe what seems right about God according to our wisdom, or are we to humbly accept the plain teaching of God's Word? Arminians inform us what is "thinkable" about God and what God "would" or "would not" do. But the problem is that what they say is unthinkable happens to be the very thing taught by the apostle Paul—not to mention Peter, John, Isaiah, and numerous other biblical writers, as well as Jesus. What Arminians say God "would never" do, the Bible says He does.

Reformed Christians affirm that God elects some to salvation "unconditionally," but this does not mean that He does so arbitrarily. Paul addresses this while confronting the very objection that predestination is unfair: "What shall we say then? Is there injustice on God's part?" Whenever we find that an objection we are raising is confronted directly in the Bible, we should be careful to heed the answer. Paul says, "By no means!" (Rom. 9:14).

Paul's answer to the question of fairness in unconditional election is important. Essentially, he replies, "Did you say *justice?*" If justice is what we want—if we want to be treated fairly by God—then the result will be the damnation of us all. No one who wants things to be fair with God can ever hope for heaven, for the simple reason that fairness demands that all sinners be damned. No, says Paul, when it comes to predestination—or salvation in general—the right category is mercy. And mercy, by definition, is sovereignly granted. It cannot be earned. It never is a matter of fairness, but always is a gift of grace. Paul elaborates in Romans 9:15–16: "For he says to Moses, 'I will have mercy on whom I have mercy, and I will have compassion on whom I have compassion.' So then it depends not on human will or exertion, but on God, who has mercy."

This makes the essential point that when the Bible speaks of God's predestination, or unconditional election, it is always joined to His mercy. Why is that? Paul's illustration from the life of Moses makes it clear. God's statement, "I will have mercy on whom I have mercy," was made after the Israelites had soiled themselves with the golden calf while Moses was receiving the law on Mount Sinai. They all were under judgment. But in this hopeless situation, God told Moses that He would choose some to be objects of His mercy. This is exactly how it is with the entire human race. The Reformed doctrine of predestination does not teach that God looked down on a neutral mass of humanity and decided to send some to heaven and others to hell. God was not sitting in eternity with a pile of daisies, picking petals and musing, "I love him, I love him not!" Rather, God looked down from on high on humanity wholly lost in sin. When God predestined to salvation, He predestined sinners who were bound for judgment and were utterly opposed to His will. Donald Grey Barnhouse therefore states: "If we may say so, the doctrine of election was God's secret weapon which made it possible for some men to be saved. If He had not retreated into

His sovereignty . . . there would have been nothing but a curse and no one would have been saved."[11]

The reason unconditional election is not ruled out by the charge of unfairness is that it is guided by mercy and not justice. It is unconditional because nothing could be found in us to commend us to God's choice. Instead, election is based solely on something in God: His sovereign mercy. How important it is for the believer in Christ to learn this truth, for it says that if we have been saved through faith then our salvation is grounded not on anything in ourselves—not even our faith, which is God's gift to the elect (Eph. 2:9)—but on the unchangeable will of God as guided by His sovereign mercy. As Paul states, "So then it depends not on human will or exertion, but on God, who has mercy. . . . [for] he has mercy on whomever he wills, and he hardens whomever he wills" (Rom. 9:16, 18).

But what about poor Pharaoh? Paul says that "the Scripture says to Pharaoh, 'For this very purpose I have raised you up, that I might show my power in you, and that my name might be proclaimed in all the earth'" (Rom. 9:17). How could that be fair to Pharaoh? First, remember that when God hardened Pharaoh, he was already a guilty sinner. God sovereignly chose not to show him mercy but gave him a just judgment—his repeatedly hardened heart—so as to display His power in Pharaoh's destruction. But Paul also says that God "raised up" Pharaoh for this purpose. We must affirm that it was according to God's sovereign purpose that Pharaoh existed in the first place; God had foreordained that Pharaoh would perish in his sin. This does not remove Pharaoh's judgment for his sin, which he willingly committed. As the potter has every right to make vessels of clay for whatever use he desires, God the Creator has the right to raise up reprobates such as Pharaoh to serve His purposes, including the purpose of displaying the glory of His power and wrath.

Objection # 2: Who Blames Them?

This leads to the second classic objection to predestination, which argues that reprobates cannot be blamed for their sin since God decided everything in advance. This happens to be the second objection that Paul considers in Romans 9: "You will say to me then, 'Why does he still find fault? For who can resist his will?'" (v. 19).

At this point, if we are expecting a cooperative reply from the apostle, we are going to be disappointed. Paul responds, "But who are you, O man, to answer back to God?" (Rom. 9:20). We are reminded of God's reply to Job when that suffering saint saw fit to question God's designs. God responded, "Who is this that darkens counsel by words without knowledge?" (Job 38:2). God went on to ask Job where he was "when the morning stars sang together" (Job 38:7) and when all the rest of the universe came into being in all the splendor of God's creation glory.

The point is that man is not in a position to question the fitness of God's perfect will. The way for us to treat profitably with God is to take the position finally assumed by Job when the Lord was finished with him: "Behold, I am of small account; what shall I answer you? I lay my hand on my mouth" (Job 40:4).

Paul calls us to accept that because we are His creatures, God the Creator has every right to do with us whatever He wills: "Will what is molded say to its molder, 'Why have you made me like this?' Has the potter no right over the clay, to make out of the same lump one vessel for honored use and another for dishonorable use?" (Rom. 9:20–21). Just as a human potter may make a vase or a chamber pot out of a lump of clay, so God made man out of the dust. What He chooses to make out of this vessel or that one is His business.

At this point Paul makes what I consider to be one of the most difficult statements on the topic of election—indeed, one of the most challenging passages in the entire Bible: "What if God, desiring to show his wrath and to make known his power, has endured with much patience vessels of wrath prepared for destruction, in order to make known the riches of his glory for vessels of mercy, which he has prepared beforehand for glory—even us whom he has called, not from the Jews only but also from the Gentiles?" (Rom. 9:22–24). What does this say? It says, "If it sounds like God has created some people to be saved into eternal glory but has also created others to be condemned in eternal damnation, what of it?"

We may reply, "But God is supposed to be good, and a good God would never make people simply to be condemned!" That is the Arminian position in a nutshell, as we previously saw. But how does the Bible reply? Does Paul say, "Well, if you don't think that's right or good, then God will be happy to conform to your opinion"? Is that what we would like? If we know the truth about ourselves and the worthiness of our opinions, we will not want that. Neither does the eternal, holy, exalted Creator God have the slightest intention of conforming to our expectations and demands. What He says instead is that we should reconsider what we think regarding the greatest good. We are humanists, so we consider the highest well-being of the most humans to constitute the highest good, above even the glory of God's justice, wrath, and power. But God is a theist! And He thinks that the highest good is the fullest display of His own glory. So the question is, who is right? The theist or the humanist? God or man? Paul does not even bother to elaborate the answer.

Paul flatly states that for the sake of the display of "his wrath and to make known his power," God "prepared" certain people "for destruction" (Rom. 9:22). He also "endured with much patience" their willful unbelief and sin, all while showering them with blessings in this wonderful world He made for us. But through their rebellion and subsequent judgment, God ordained that the glories of the perfection of His power, justice, holiness, and wrath would be displayed forever.

Meanwhile, God prepared others—"even us whom he has called, not from the Jews only but also from the Gentiles"—that is, those who believe on the Lord Jesus Christ and are saved, "in order to make known the riches of his glory for vessels of mercy, which he has prepared beforehand for glory" (Rom. 9:23). What does this mean? It means that God ordains the condemnation of the reprobate not only to show forth His justice and wrath, but also to display His mercy and grace to us, who equally deserve hell but receive salvation instead.

Barnhouse tells of a shop in Paris that is world-famous for its magnificent, intricate white lace. To display their samples in the store windows, the proprietors place the darkest black velvet behind the lace; only in this way can the intricate details of the craftsmen's achievement be seen. It is the same with God's grace. Were no one ever condemned—were there no display of God's judgment and wrath—there would be no knowledge of the glories of God's grace. In that case, the true God would be unknown to His creatures, and His purpose in creation—to display the fullness of His glory—would be unrealized. Having failed in this purpose, God would no longer be God. For this reason, God's decree of reprobation is necessary. God being perfect in every attribute, it is necessary for His every attribute to be exercised: goodness in creation, power in triumph, mercy in grace, and justice in wrath.

What's So Great about Unconditional Election?

Thus, we see Paul's teaching on unconditional election, which is consistent with the Bible's whole teaching. But there is one last question that may plague troubled minds: "We see that this is what the Bible states, though we struggle to accept it. But why do some of you seem to love this doctrine so much?" In other words, "What's so great about the doctrine of unconditional election?" Let me answer with four points that I hope will be helpful.

First, *unconditional election promotes humility and not pride.* This is the opposite of what some people surmise. They imagine that if I believe I am chosen by God, I must think I am somehow special and superior. But unconditional election ascribes salvation not to any merit in the Christian. It fully embraces the Bible's teaching of our total depravity. It says that unless salvation is wholly of God then I could not be saved, so great is my sin and enmity to the things of God. As Arthur Pink comments:

> The truth of God's sovereignty . . . removes every ground for human boasting and instills the spirit of humility in its stead. It declares that salvation is of the Lord—of the Lord in its origination, in its operation, and in its consummation. . . . And all this is most humbling to the heart of man, who wants to contribute something to the price of his redemption and do that which will afford ground for boasting and self-satisfaction.[12]

Where is the ground for human boasting when we realize that our salvation is in spite of our utter unworthiness and solely because of God's sovereign grace? Our great need is to have our pride and self-reliance laid low. It is precisely this doctrine of sovereign election that humbles the believer's heart.

Second, the Bible emphasizes that *unconditional election promotes holiness and not license*. This, too, seems counterintuitive. After all, if my salvation is caused not by my own effort but by God's mercy, then what motive have I to press on with the difficult work of sanctification?

This question reveals a gross misunderstanding of salvation as a whole. It fails to realize that holiness is the goal for which we are saved. It is God's purpose in our salvation that we should be holy, and therefore those who are predestined to salvation are predestined to holiness. This was Paul's emphasis in Ephesians 1:4: "He chose us . . . that we should be holy and blameless before him." When God elected sinners, He elected them *to holiness*, so that holiness is the particular mark of the elect. Paul writes elsewhere, "For this is the will of God, your sanctification" (1 Thess. 4:3).

This is the great priority of the Christian life—not happiness, but holiness. Knowing that God has predestined us to personal holiness is a great motivation to pursue the same. If we thought our growth in holiness arose from our own desire and effort, what hopelessness that would produce. But now we find that long before the worlds were formed, God elected that we would be holy. What does this mean but that we *will* be holy? If we are in Christ, we can be sure of it. Knowing that this is our destiny as Christians, we find courage to embrace it and become what we are meant to be, and we are thus emboldened to a more active faith.

Third, unconditional election is a great and beloved doctrine because *it promotes assurance of salvation but not presumption*. The Bible establishes salvation on the basis of saving faith in Jesus Christ. No one who does not display credible faith in Christ should ever think himself elect. Election, like salvation, is only "in Christ." But what a comfort it is to know that if I do believe in Christ, the Bible tells me I was chosen by God from before the foundation of the world.

Here is where the doctrine of election so greatly helps. It tells us that if we can say to God that we trust in Jesus, then God tells us our faith is grounded on the solid rock of His eternal election. We are not saved by believing we are elect; rather, we realize that we are elect because we have faith in Christ. Faith assures us that we are secure in God's eternally strong hands. How many Christians stumble on in weakness, burdened with doubts that would be erased if only they knew their salvation rested not in themselves but in God? Election tells us that it was God who sought us and not we who sought Him, that God called us to Himself because He chose us long ago. I don't know about you, but that changes everything in my struggle for assurance of salvation, and therefore gives me peace about my eternal soul. Calvin speaks with characteristic understatement when he writes: "If we find no certainty in things on earth, we must know that our salvation rests upon God, and that He holds it in such a manner that it can never vanish away. This is a happy consideration."[13]

Fourth, *the doctrine of unconditional election promotes glory to God alone and not to man.* Since our salvation "depends not on human will or exertion, but on God, who has mercy" (Rom. 9:16), then all the glory for our salvation belongs to Him. As Jonah 2:9 (NIV) says, "Salvation comes from the LORD," and therefore all our praise is His alone.

Are you willing to admit that in you there is no reason for hope, and that there is nothing in you that marks you out as different from the great mass of unbelieving humanity? Do you agree that you have nothing of your own to commend you, and unless God should show mercy to you despite your sin—before all creation and in Christ and all to the praise of His sovereign grace alone—there is no way that you could be saved? If you cannot say this, if you recoil from the sovereign and electing grace of God, then on what are you really relying? Must you not necessarily be cherishing some merit of your own, some strength in you that you believe will win you through to heaven? Listen: there is no peace in that, and the Bible offers you neither hope nor assurance nor joy in such a faith. Instead, let us agree with the lines written by James Montgomery Boice shortly before his death: "Since grace is the source of the life that is mine, and faith is a gift from on high / I'll boast in my Savior, all merit decline, and glorify God 'til I die."[14]

Around the time he wrote that hymn, Boice received a letter from a man who had heard him teaching the doctrine of predestination. The man admitted his horror when he first heard it and stated that he bent all his will toward disproving the doctrine. But his attitude changed on the day that his father died. It was then that he understood the Bible's teaching on total depravity, that man is dead in sin and helpless to do anything meriting salvation. The man wrote:

> I was at my father's side and holding his hand when he took his final breath. . . . I did not call the nurse in for approximately twenty minutes. During that time I sat next to his body. There was absolutely no life in it and I was helpless to do anything to change that fact. I began to think about Ephesians 2. We were dead in transgressions and sins. . . . The account of Jesus raising Lazarus from the dead came to my mind. . . . Lazarus would respond to nothing other than the voice of Jesus. . . . [T]he passages

kept coming. . . . Well, needless to say, I was convinced. For the first time in my life I understood the true significance of . . . election. . . . I was overwhelmed by God's grace. Why would he choose me? When I realized it was because He is sovereign and not because He saw anything . . . in me . . . , I was overwhelmed by His grace. Truly the wonder of wonders is that God chooses to save anyone.[15]

Our problem with predestination is not that the doctrine is questionable to sanctified minds. Our problem is that we resist the truth about ourselves. When we realize that no one could be saved by God's justice and that His mercy is by its very nature sovereignly distributed, and recognize that our faith in Christ reveals that God chose us despite our demerit by His simple, sovereign grace, then we will see what a great doctrine this is. But more than that, we will start to glory in the perfection and the majesty and the wonder of God's grace for us. And we will ascribe all glory to Him with unspeakable joy.

4

WHAT'S SO GREAT ABOUT LIMITED ATONEMENT?

HEBREWS 12:2

✛   ✛   ✛

Who for the joy that was set before him endured the
cross, despising the shame. (Heb. 12:2)

EVERY FAMILY HAS A BLACK SHEEP. It is that brother or uncle or cousin who has to be acknowledged as a family member but who is, frankly, a bit embarrassing. As we consider the family of letters that make up the Reformed acrostic, TULIP, allow me to introduce the black sheep: L—limited atonement. As is always the case with black sheep, it is hard for us to deny L its place in the family; after all, without the L, the acrostic no longer spells our beloved Dutch flower. But there are always those who insist the black sheep doesn't really belong. There must have been a mistake: the babies must have been switched at the hospital or the FedEx driver must have delivered the wrong package. This is the kind of thing jokingly whispered at the family dinner table; it accounts for the so-called "four-point Calvinists" who do not want limited atonement in the family portrait.

I have performed funerals for black sheep, and it is usually hard to know what to say, especially when we're pretty sure he or she wasn't a Christian. Everyone knows that you don't have much to work with and are just doing your best. This is how I feel when I hear many Reformed scholars defending limited atonement. They are searching for positive things to say and hoping to make it through without doing too much harm.

Well, let me assure you, I am not writing to deliver a funeral oration for limited atonement. In fact, I would like to reverse the famous line from Mark Antony's eulogy for Julius Caesar, as immortalized by Shakespeare: "I have come not to bury limited atonement, but to praise it." Indeed, I want to do my part to rehabilitate the reputation of our dear relation, limited atonement, proclaiming it to be not a black sheep in the family of Reformed doctrine, but a teaching worthy of our high esteem and a privileged place at the table of our hearts.

My text is not one of those classically assigned to this debate, but rather the remarkable statement made by the writer of Hebrews about the death of our Lord. Hebrews 12:2 tells us to fix our eyes on Jesus, the author and perfecter of our faith, "who for the joy that was set before him endured the cross, despising the shame." We don't often think of Jesus taking up the cross with joy in His heart, but the Bible says He did. So I want to pose the question: what was the joy in Jesus' heart as He scorned the shame of the cross? To answer this question rightly is both to understand and to appreciate the doctrine of limited atonement.

The Divine Intent for the Atonement

We know that it was Jesus' delight to do His Father's will, and this undoubtedly formed part of His joy as He faced the cross. The first question to ask about limited atonement, then, is the divine *intent* of the cross. What was God's stated purpose in the atoning death of His Son, in which Jesus rejoiced? Did the Father intend for His Son to die generally for all humanity? If so, did God intend actually to save them all or merely to provide them all with the opportunity for salvation? The first of these options is the universal view and the second is the Arminian view. Or, as the Reformed view has it, was God's intent for the atonement limited to His own elect?

Those who embrace the authority of the Bible rule out the universal view, since the Bible clearly teaches that not all people will be saved. In contrast, the Arminian teaching of universal atonement is undoubtedly the most popular among evangelicals. But was it God's design that Christ should die equally for all people, rendering them not saved but salvable? Was it God's intent to provide salvation for all through the death of Christ, though not to apply it to all? Many scholars today hold this view; recent books by Millard Erickson, Donald Bloesch, and Bruce Demarest have taken this position. Demarest writes: "Scripture leads us to conclude that God loves all people he created and that Christ died to provide salvation for all. . . . By divine *intention* Christ's suffering and death are universal in its provision."[16]

Let us admit that this proposal sounds attractive to our ears, at least at first. But is it biblical to say that God's intent for the atoning work of Christ extends generally and equally to all people? The Reformed view says that it is not, for according to Scripture the atonement was intended for the elect only. Despite the loving attitude of God toward the world, according to the Bible the intent of His Son's death was limited to (or particular to) the elect. Isaiah prophesied, "He was cut off out of the land of the living, stricken for the transgression *of my people*" (Isa. 53:8). The angel told Joseph, "You shall call his name Jesus, for he will save *his people* from their sins" (Matt. 1:21). Jesus explained, "The Son of Man came not to be served but to serve, and to give his life as a ransom *for many*" (Matt. 20:28). "I am the good shepherd," he preached. "The good shepherd lays down his life for *the sheep*" (John 10:11, emphasis added in all cited verses).

One of the Reformed arguments against universal atonement, or general redemption, as it is sometimes called, is that it sees God's sovereign intention frustrated by the will of man. John Owen, in his seminal treatment of limited atonement, points out the sequence of Arminian reasoning. First, "Christ died for all and every one, elect and reprobate." But second, "Most of them for whom Christ died are damned."[17] According to this view, most of the people for whom Christ offered atonement do not have their sins atoned for. If God intended the salvation of all, His intention clearly failed. John Murray observes:

The very nature of Christ's mission and accomplishment is involved in this question. Did Christ come to make the salvation of all men possible, to remove obstacles that stood in the way of salvation, and merely to make provision for salvation? Or did he come to save his people? . . . Did he come to make men redeemable? Or did he come effectually and infallibly to redeem? The doctrine of the atonement must be radically revised if, as atonement, it applies to those who finally perish as well as to those who are the heirs of eternal life. In that event we should have to dilute the grand categories in terms of which the Scripture defines the atonement and deprive them of their most precious import and glory.[18]

The Effect of Christ's Atoning Work

This leads to the second question about Christ's atoning work. Undoubtedly, Jesus faced the cross with joy not only because He was obeying the Father's will, but also because of the results of what He was about to do. What, then, was the *effect* of Christ's death? Did His death bring about the salvation of all sinners, including those who never believe? Again, all evangelicals reject such a teaching, since we know that not all are saved. But did the cross achieve merely the possibility of salvation for all mankind, as Arminians insist? Or did the atonement actually effect the salvation of those for whom Jesus died, namely, the elect, as taught by Reformed theology?

Perhaps this is the place to point out that the word *limited* gives many people problems with the Reformed position on the atonement. With all black sheep, there is usually one particular issue that causes the embarrassment. Some just can't hold jobs, while others drink too much or are obnoxious in public. Here, the word *limited* just doesn't seem to go well with *atonement*. It makes it appear that we don't think highly of the atonement of Christ, when really we do. This rhetorical weakness accounts for the desire of many to rename the doctrine more positively, such as "particular redemption."

But it is helpful to note that both Arminians and Calvinists believe in limited atonement. The question is with regard to *what* is limited. Arminians believe that the atonement is limited in terms of its efficacy. Calvinists believe the atonement is limited in the scope of people for whom it was intended. Arminians believe the atonement is unlimited in scope but limited in effect: it offers everyone the chance of salvation. Calvinists believe the atonement is limited in scope but unlimited in effect: it effectually saves the elect. If we think of the atonement as a bridge spanning a great river, Arminians see it as infinitely wide, but not reaching all the way to the far bank; Calvinists hold that the atonement is a narrow bridge, wide enough only for the elect, but reaching all the way to the other side. We believe that Christ's death actually saves those for whom He died.

The Arminians' denial of limited atonement is mainly an application of their prior rejection of unconditional election, since it is election that undergirds particular redemption. But this denial of election becomes especially troubling when it touches on the atonement. Not only do Arminians posit that God's intention to save all mankind is frustrated by human unbelief. They go on to say that Christ did not really save anyone by dying on the cross—indeed, He might have died in vain, saving no one.

But how far such ideas are from the biblical teaching of the efficacy of Christ's atoning death. Surely the idea that Christ died for everyone in general but no one in particular is foreign to the book of Hebrews, for it would have meant that Christ faced the cross with anxiety rather than joy. But Hebrews insists that Jesus "entered once for all into the holy places . . . by means of his own blood, thus securing an eternal redemption" (Heb. 9:12). Jesus faced the cross with joy because of the salvation He thus secured. Peter takes a similar view: "He himself bore our sins in his body on the tree, that we might die to sin and live to righteousness" (1 Peter 2:24). Jesus actually bore "our" sins, paying the penalty in our place.

As Murray argued, if Christ's death was limited in its achievement, all the great biblical words to describe the effect of the cross are emptied of their saving significance. The Bible speaks of Christ's achievement in terms of propitiation (Rom. 3:25), reconciliation (2 Cor. 5:18–19), atonement (Heb. 2:17, NIV), and redemption (1 Peter 1:18–19, NIV; Gal. 3:13). But to the Arminian, this propitiation does not really propitiate (that is, it does not truly turn away God's wrath); Christ's reconciliation does not necessarily reconcile; and the atoning work does not effectually make sinners at one with God. J. I. Packer thus writes that the Arminian doctrine of universal atonement, "so far from magnifying the love and grace of God, dishonors both it and Him, for it reduces God's love to an impotent wish and turns the whole economy of 'saving' grace, so called . . . into a monumental divine failure. . . . So far from magnifying the merit and worth of Christ's death, it cheapens it, for it makes Christ die in vain."[19]

Arminian doctrine especially confuses the idea of redemption, preaching that Christ's death has unlocked the bars of our cells, but that it takes our faith to open the doors. Or Arminians say that Jesus has placed the infinite value of His blood into the bank for everyone; by faith, we must go and open our account. However, Christ did not offer the payment of His blood to us, but to the justice of God. In the Arminian view, God has received the payment for the debt of everyone's sins, yet He still holds most people under wrath. The Arminian view of universal atonement therefore not only confuses the categories of salvation, but presents an affront to the justice of God. James Montgomery Boice and Philip Ryken observe: "If there is a real redemption, then the person who has been redeemed must be set free. When the Bible says that Jesus redeemed us by his death on the Cross, that redemption must be an effective redemption, and those who have been redeemed must be actual beneficiaries of it."[20]

To be sure, Calvinists agree that Christ's death secured many blessings generally applied to the whole world, though we deny that atonement was one of them. It is because of Christ's death that reprobates today are not already in hell, as the gospel is still going forth in the world. Christ's death secures the free offer of salvation to all peoples, an inestimable benefit. Christ's death has inaugurated His reign, so that Christians have brought His mercy and grace to every arena of life, founding the world's hospitals and schools, and even laying the foundation for scientific progress. All these blessings and more flow from the cross. But Christ's actual *atoning* work was not given generally to all, but rather was efficaciously limited to the redeemed.

Arminian "Problem Texts"

This is probably the right time to address the main Arminian argument: the many verses that seem to insist on a universal atonement. We may place these "problem texts" into three categories. First are those that seem to teach that God wills the salvation of all people. An example is 1 Timothy 2:3–4, where Paul says that God "desires all people to be saved and to come to the knowledge of the truth." But who are these "all"? Going back to the start of the chapter, we see that Paul means all kinds or classes of people. He asks his readers to pray "for all people," such as "kings and all who are in high positions" (1 Tim. 2:1–2). Similarly, Hebrews 2:9 says that Christ would "taste death for everyone." But this must be understood in terms of that chapter's focus on those who are Christ's "brothers" (Heb. 2:11), that is, the elect, whom He calls "the children God has given me" (Heb. 2:13).

A second class of statements suggests that some for whom Christ died are ultimately lost. Paul warns believers not to cause weaker Christians to stumble by their exercise of Christian liberty, so that "by your knowledge this weak person is destroyed, the brother for whom Christ died" (1 Cor. 8:11). But Paul is not speaking of the weaker Christians being lost, but of their well-being being assaulted. A stronger verse is 2 Peter 2:1, where the apostle warns against "false teachers among you, who will secretly bring in destructive heresies, even denying the Master who bought them." Arminians claim that this seals the case against five-point Calvinism, since it proves that even unbelieving heretics were purchased by the blood of Christ. In reply, we point out that the weight of biblical testimony should not be revised by this one verse; rather we should understand the ambiguous verse in terms of the whole testimony of Scripture. Here, it seems that Peter is referring to what the false teachers claimed for themselves, rather than what was actually the case.

The third category of supposed "problem texts" includes those that speak of salvation for the "world." John the Baptist cried, "Behold, the Lamb of God, who takes away the sin of the world" (John 1:29). The newly converted Samaritans said of Jesus, "We know that this is indeed the Savior of the world" (John 4:42). And John exclaimed, "He is the propitiation for our sins, and not for ours only but also for the sins of the whole world" (1 John 2:2). How, in light of these verses, can Calvinists persist in denying a universal atonement? The answer is by considering John's use of the word *world*. In many cases, John does speak of the "world" (Greek, *kosmos*) as the unbelieving world in opposition to God. But in speaking of the benefits of salvation, he consistently contrasts the world with Jewish exclusivity.

This is clearly what the Samaritans, the objects of such Jewish scorn, had in mind. Salvation was not merely for Jews, but for Gentiles, too—in other words, the whole world.

Therefore, under thoughtful consideration, the Arminian problem texts do not present a true problem. Despite the rhetorical advantage gained by appeal to isolated texts without reference to their context, the Arminian teaching simply cannot account for the whole testimony of Scripture. Meanwhile, Calvinists, starting with the overwhelming biblical description of Christ's atoning work, and consulting the context in which the "problem verses" are found, can account for all of the Bible. Murray comments:

> It is easy for the proponents of universal atonement to make offhand appeal to a few texts. But this method is not worthy of the serious student of Scripture. It is necessary for us to discover what redemption or atonement really means. And when we examine the Scripture we find that the glory of the cross of Christ is bound up with the effectiveness of its accomplishment. Christ redeemed us to God by his blood, he gave himself a ransom that he might deliver us from all iniquity. The atonement is efficacious substitution.[21]

The Objects of Christ's Atoning Work

Third, when we ask what was the joy set before Jesus as He took up the cross, we must consider the *objects* for whom He died.

Did Jesus rejoice at what He was going to do equally for every person in the world, many if not most of whom would perish in hell, or did He rejoice over the salvation He was procuring for those precious souls known to God in eternity and given Him as His own bride?

By consulting the Bible, we find that Christ endured His death not generally for all people; rather, its effectual benefits were directed to a limited number of people. Who, then, are these "many" (Matt. 20:28)? In a great passage that teaches many Calvinistic doctrines, Jesus describes these people in two ways. First, the many are those who believe in Him: "I am the bread of life; whoever comes to me shall not hunger, and whoever believes in me shall never thirst" (John 6:35). But He then immediately describes them from the divine perspective: "All that the Father gives me will come to me, and whoever comes to me I will never cast out. . . . And this is the will of him who sent me, that I should lose nothing of all that he has given me, but raise it up on the last day" (John 6:37, 39). In other words, these believers are none other than God's elect, whom the Father gave to His Son from all eternity, for whom Jesus suffered and died, and who will certainly attain to everlasting life in His love.

Perhaps most pointedly, on the night of His arrest, Jesus prayed, "Glorify your Son that the Son may glorify you, since you have given him authority over all flesh, to give eternal life *to all whom you have given him*" (John 17:1–2, emphasis added). Here we see Jesus interceding on behalf of those for whom He was about to die. We have asked, for whom did Jesus rejoice at the cross? To make the matter plain, Jesus specified those on whom His joy was set and for whom His mediatorial ministry was to be offered: "I am not praying for the world but for those whom you have given me" (John 17:9).

It is true that Jesus died for all who believe. But are they redeemed because they believe or do they believe because they were redeemed? Arminians, denying both total depravity and unconditional election, argue the former: they are redeemed because they believe. But how is an unregenerate person to believe, when Jesus says, "Unless one is born again he cannot see the kingdom of God" (John 3:3)? Calvinists therefore argue that we believe because Christ redeemed us: faith originates not in the will of man but in the saving action of God. Owen states: "Faith is itself among the principal effects and fruits of the death of Christ. . . . Christ died for us that we might believe."[22] Thus, Luke remarks about one occasion of Paul's preaching, "As many as were appointed to eternal life believed" (Acts 13:48). And Paul instructs us: "For by grace you have been saved through faith. And this is not your own doing; it is the gift of God, not a result of works, so that no one may boast" (Eph. 2:8–9).

Moreover, what are we to make of unbelief under the Arminians' scheme? For them, all our sins are paid for, except that some do not believe. Owen counters by asking: "That unbelief, is it a sin, or is it not? If it be not, how can it be a cause for damnation? If it be, Christ died for it, or He did not. If He did not, then He died not for all the sins of all men. If He did, why is this an obstacle to their salvation?"[23]

Given the teaching of the Bible, we must conclude that the Reformed doctrine of limited atonement rightly teaches that

1) God's intent for the atonement was limited to the elect, 2) Christ's atoning work was unlimited in its efficacy for His own people, and 3) Christ died specifically for those given Him by the Father, following up His death with His gift of the new birth and saving faith. How wonderful it is to realize that Jesus went to the cross with each of His individual people on His heart! He had the joy of knowing your personal salvation and mine when He took up the cross, scorning its shame. This is why, when the believer receives the bread of the Lord's Supper, he hears the same words Jesus spoke to His first disciples: "This my body, which is given for *you*" (Luke 22:19, emphasis added). Receiving the cup, each believer is told, "This cup that is poured out for *you* is the new covenant in my blood" (Luke 22:20, emphasis added).

Because many of His flock have yet to come in, Jesus appoints ministers and missionaries today to take the gospel to all the places where His people dwell. We preach and witness today with the same rationale that Jesus gave to Paul in decadent Corinth: "I have many in this city who are my people" (Acts 18:10).

What's So Great about Limited Atonement?

I am writing to praise the doctrine of limited atonement because it so exalts the cross of Jesus Christ, which gained a full redemption for all those appointed by God to eternal life. But what is the cash value of this doctrine? Does it offer something to my Christian experience or is it just abstract theology? What's so great about the doctrine of limited atonement?

First, whenever a doctrine receives the prominence the Bible gives to Christ's atonement, it must be significant to our lives. The solemnity of the subject matter of Christ's atonement urges us to consider it of great significance and to think carefully about it, in conformity with the Scriptures. In this respect, limited atonement should be received as a great doctrine simply because of its importance to Jesus and His saving work.

Second, if we grasp how personal in its application and how efficacious in its effects is the cross of Christ, we will find solid ground for our assurance of salvation. There can be no assurance if the ultimate cause of our redemption is found in ourselves. The Arminian concept of a universal atonement, Packer remarks, "destroys the Scriptural ground of assurance altogether. . . . My salvation, on this view, depends not on what Christ did for me, but on what I subsequently do for myself."[24] This is why assurance of salvation is a field of theology and Christian experience plowed only by the Reformed. Murray notes, "It is no wonder that the doctrine of assurance should have found its true expression in that theology which is conditioned by the thought of the divine atonement or effective redemption, the irreversibility of effectual calling, and the immutability of the gifts of grace."[25]

It is when you realize that even your faith is the outworking of Christ's saving death for you, by the electing will of the Father, as applied by the Spirit, that you know the solid ground on which your salvation stands. If you truly believe—and the Bible gives you tests to determine whether you do—you can rest your heart in God's sovereign grace and begin looking forward to an eternity of glory in the kingdom that you are now called to serve.

Lastly, limited atonement impacts us powerfully with regard to the psychology of our devotion to the Lord. There are some who die for principles, and we admire them for it. Socrates accepted the cup of hemlock for the principle of tacit consent to civic rule. For this, his influence has spread far and wide across the ages. There are others who die for causes. If we share the cause, we may honor the martyr's name. Nathan Hale has gone down in American history as the revolutionary who declared, "I only regret that I have but one life to lose for my country." School-children are taught those words even today, and we remember him with respect. Logically, the doctrine of universal atonement places Jesus in this category, though as the most noble of people who died for the greatest possible cause.

But there is another category of devotion that rises far above the rest. Some die for principles and others for causes. But what about someone who dies for me? This calls for a different kind of devotion altogether.

The movie *Saving Private Ryan* tells of a rescue operation immediately after the Allied invasion of Normandy in June 1944. The War Department learns that three out of four sons in a family named Ryan have died in battle on the same day. The Army's top general orders that the fourth son be rescued from behind German lines, where he parachuted on D-Day. An elite squad of Army Rangers is assigned to find Private Ryan. The search leads to a bridge where German tanks are trying to break through Allied lines, and there the squad is destroyed as the quest finally succeeds. As the captain who saved Ryan lies dying on the bridge, surrounded by the bodies of the men from his squad, he draws Ryan close and gasps: "Earn this. Earn it." The movie concludes with Ryan, as an old man, returning to the cemetery where the men who died for him were buried. Falling to his knees at Captain Miller's grave, he says to the white plaster cross: "Every day I think about what you said to me that day on the bridge. I've tried to live my life the best I could. I hope that was enough. I hope that at least in your eyes, I earned what all of you have done for me." Turning to his wife, who comes up beside him, he stammers: "Tell me I have led a good life. Tell me I'm a good man."

We praise God that we are not required to earn what Christ has done for us, for we never could do so. We receive His death by simple faith alone. Jesus never demands that we earn what He did for us. But the Bible does tell us to live "in a manner worthy of the Lord" (Col. 1:10). So we can turn to His wooden cross every day and pray, "If, with all Your glory, You, the Son of God, died for me, then I can live for You." We live not merely for a principle and not even for a great cause. We live for a person, the Lord Jesus Christ. He died not merely for a principle or even for the greatest of causes. He died for us. So every Christian can say, "I live for Him, because He died for me." He died for me.

5

What's So Great About Irresistible Grace?

Matthew 9:9

✢ ✢ ✢

As Jesus passed on from there, he saw a man called Matthew sitting at the tax booth, and he said to him, "Follow me." And he rose and followed him. (Matt. 9:9)

One of the most important insights of Reformed theology is the unity of the works of the Trinity. Calvinists believe that God the Father, God the Son, and God the Holy Spirit are united in the work of redeeming lost mankind. We do not believe that they act *against* one another or even *on* one another, but *with* one another in our salvation. For instance, Jesus did not die to convince the Father to change His attitude toward us from enmity to love. Rather, Jesus died on the cross because of the Father's love for us, as John 3:16 says: "For God so loved the world that he gave his only Son, that whoever believes in him should not perish but have eternal life." The Father and Son are united in their work for the salvation of those who believe: the Father electing and sending His Son; the Son atoning for the sins of those chosen and given to Him by the Father (John 6:37–40). The same harmony exists between the Son and the Spirit. Jesus did not die for the sins of all people, only to have the Holy Spirit apply the benefits of His work merely to some. Rather, the Holy Spirit regenerates precisely the people for whom Jesus offered His atoning death, so that the work of the second and third persons of the Trinity harmonizes perfectly.

This emphasis on the unity of the Trinity in salvation may be seen in the doctrines of grace as organized by the TULIP acrostic. The doctrines of grace start with a problem: T—man's *total depravity*. The answer to this problem is brought about by the unified work of the Trinity. It begins with *unconditional election*, which is focused on the Father's sovereign purpose in predestination. Salvation is then accomplished by the atoning work of Jesus on the cross, which, according to *limited atonement*, was offered for those elected by the Father. This salvation is then sovereignly applied to those same elect individuals by the regenerating work of the Holy Spirit, which is the point of *irresistible grace*. Therefore, just as unconditional election describes the grace of the Father and limited atonement describes the grace of the Son, irresistible grace presents the grace of the Holy Spirit. While acknowledging that where one member of the

Trinity acts, all are involved, we may identify irresistible grace as the Holy Spirit's own doctrine of grace.

Irresistible Grace in the Calling of Matthew

There are many examples of irresistible grace in God's Word. Perhaps most plain is the calling of the disciple Matthew, also known as Levi the tax collector. The apostle records his own conversion in his Gospel: "As Jesus passed on from there, he saw a man called Matthew sitting at the tax booth, and he said to him, 'Follow me.' And he rose and followed him" (Matt. 9:9).

Consideration of this verse makes clear the basic teaching of irresistible grace. The Lord Jesus had just returned to Capernaum from His missionary visit to the region of the Gadarenes. Capernaum had become His Galilean headquarters, and many of His most spectacular miracles already had occurred there. Seeing Matthew at his tax collector's booth, Jesus went to him and called, "Follow me." At these words, the tax collector immediately was transformed into a disciple. It is a striking illustration of God's sovereignty in salvation.

For his part, Matthew presents an equally striking picture of man's total depravity. The statement that he was "sitting at the tax booth" is loaded with meaning. At the time, there hardly could have been a more depraved person than a tax collector. The Roman Empire took bids for the right to collect taxes. These agents paid a set amount to Rome, but could keep all the rest that they collected. Tax collectors enriched themselves by preying on impoverished people, stifling trade, and operating what amounted to a local mafia. To make matters worse, they were despised for collaborating with the foreign power that had subjected their own people to bondage.

By remaining in this occupation in Capernaum, Jesus' base of operations at the time, Matthew showed his hardness of heart to the presence and preaching of Christ. Tax collectors' booths were in the most public places; Matthew's was most likely situated either at the docks by the lake or along the main road leading into town. He probably had seen and heard Jesus many times, and was well aware of some of Jesus' greatest works. Just recently, a paralytic had been cured after his friends lowered him before Jesus through a hole they made in the roof of the building where Jesus was preaching. Earlier, Jesus had cast out demons and healed multitudes of hopelessly diseased people right there in Capernaum. But none of this had had the slightest effect on Matthew. There he was in his booth, carrying on his business without any visible response to all these affairs.

In short, there was nothing in Matthew to explain his sudden willingness to believe and follow Jesus. Instead, the answer is seen in the irresistible grace of God, as the Holy Spirit applied Jesus' call with sovereign and divine power.

This helps make clear that when we speak of irresistible grace, we do not mean that God's grace is never resisted. Those who oppose this doctrine make much of the many instances when men and women shun God's grace and turn away, just as Matthew had done many times. But this objection misses the point, for the simple reason that the doctrine of irresistible grace speaks of the operation of grace in the *conversion* of sinners. We do not teach that no one resists God's grace. But we do insist that when a sinner turns to Christ in faith and begins to follow Him, this conversion is the result of the sovereign, effectual, and irresistible operation of God's grace through the ministry of the Holy Spirit.

As the conversion of Matthew shows, irresistible grace is joined to the saving call of God in Christ. Reformed theology makes an important and useful distinction between two kinds of calls. There is the general call of Christ to all the world, offered to all people irrespective of God's election. "Come to me, all who labor and are heavy laden, and I will give you rest," Jesus cried (Matt. 11:28). John records that during the Feast of Tabernacles in Jerusalem, "Jesus stood up and cried out, 'If anyone thirsts, let him come to me and drink'" (John 7:37). This is Christ's general call to anyone and everyone who hears. It is a sincere call and offer of salvation. But because of man's totally depraved state, no one answers this call by his or her own volition. Indeed, no one can. This was Matthew's situation. For all the many times he had seen and heard Jesus, for all that he had learned about what Jesus was doing, and in spite of even direct appeals to faith that Matthew very well may have heard, his sinful heart was indisposed to answer. Jesus once explained this, saying, "No one can come to me unless the Father who sent me draws him" (John 6:44). The sinful heart is hostile to God and uninterested in His offer of salvation; Matthew modeled this perfectly as he greedily went on extorting people in the very presence of Christ's saving ministry.

On one occasion, when Jesus was describing the impossibility of a rich man ever entering God's kingdom, Peter asked in dismay, "Who then can be saved?" (Matt. 19:25). This is a good question that arises naturally when we honestly face what the Bible says about man's hopeless condition in sin. The Bible describes unregenerate sinners as spiritually dead, blind, and enslaved. So how *can* anyone be converted to faith in Christ? The answer is another kind of call, one that comes with divine power to bring us to Christ: the effectual call. As Jesus told Peter, "With man this is impossible, but with God all things are possible" (Matt. 19:26).

Conversion to Christ is not only possible, but happens by virtue of His effectual call, by which the Holy Spirit works with saving power to bring the unbelieving sinner to faith. R. C. Sproul explains: "The unregenerate experience the outward call of the gospel. This outward call will not effect salvation unless the call is heard and embraced in faith. Effectual calling refers to the work of the Holy Spirit in regeneration. Here the call is within. The regenerate are called inwardly. Everyone who receives the inward call of regeneration responds in faith."[26] As John Murray writes of this saving call of God, "since it is effectual, [it] carries with it the operative grace whereby the person called is enabled to answer the call and to embrace Jesus Christ as he is freely offered in the gospel."[27]

The effectual call offers the only realistic explanation for what happened to Matthew. He did not get up from his tax collector's seat because he summoned up the will to change his mind about Jesus. Rather, he came because Christ called him effectually, as the Holy Spirit applied the saving grace of God to his soul. Through the effectual call, not only was he enabled to respond in faith, but a change took place in his heart so that he was compelled to do so. God's grace was irresistible in his conversion precisely because it was a sovereign and divine act whereby God saved his soul. If a king or a queen is able to summon his or her subjects at a word, how much more is the almighty God able to call His chosen people to follow Jesus. For this reason, when called by the voice of God in Christ, Matthew "rose and followed him."

A Biblical Defense of Irresistible Grace

Simply put, the doctrine of irresistible grace states that sinners are converted to faith in Christ because the sovereign God extends His almighty power to change their hearts through the gospel. Ezekiel spoke of this, saying: "I will give you a new heart, and a new spirit I will put within you. And I will remove the heart of stone from your flesh and give you a heart of flesh" (Ezek. 36:26). Jesus, too, explained it: "All that the Father gives me will come to me, and whoever comes to me I will never cast out" (John 6:37).

Indeed, many lines of biblical reasoning call for our acceptance of irresistible grace. First there is the necessary implication of unconditional election and limited atonement. If God has sovereignly predestined certain people to salvation, then it is necessary that those people actually be saved through faith in Christ. The salvation of the elect does not depend on their own willingness, but is accomplished as a sovereign act of God in conformity to the sovereign plan of God. Luke states this matter-of-factly in describing the salvation of those who heard Paul preaching the gospel. He writes, "As many as were appointed to eternal life believed" (Acts 13:48).

Moreover, if Jesus died not merely to make salvation possible for everyone but actually to save His own people, then the salvation of the elect cannot be decided by the willingness of corrupt, unregenerate sinners to place their trust in Him. Instead, Jesus said, "My sheep hear my voice, and I know them, and they follow me" (John 10:27). It is by the effectual working of the Holy Spirit in irresistible grace that the elect hear Christ's voice and follow. Jesus added that the converse is also true; speaking to unbelieving Jews, He said, "You do not believe because you are not part of my flock" (John 10:26). In short, if God's grace is wholly sovereign in election and in atonement, then grace also must be wholly sovereign in conversion.

Second, it is clear from the Bible that the Spirit's regenerating work always precedes and causes faith. Jesus stated this to Nicodemus: "Unless one is born again he cannot see the kingdom of God" (John 3:3). This is reflected more or less clearly in every conversion recorded in the New Testament. An excellent example is the conversion of Lydia, which Luke records by writing, "The Lord opened her heart to pay attention to what was said by Paul" (Acts 16:14). Likewise, Jesus ascribed Peter's great confession not to the operations of his flesh but to divine grace: "Flesh and blood has not revealed this to you, but my Father who is in heaven" (Matt. 16:17).

Regeneration—the new birth—precedes faith, so that prior to being born again it is impossible for anyone to believe on Jesus. Paul explains why: "The natural person does not accept the things of the Spirit of God, for they are folly to him, and he is not able to understand them because they are spiritually discerned" (1 Cor. 2:14). Therefore, if regeneration had to result from faith—if unregenerate sinners had to believe in order to be saved—then according to Paul, no one would ever be regenerated and saved. Instead, the Bible uniformly teaches what our sinful condition demands: regeneration precedes and causes saving faith. The apostle John put it succinctly: "Everyone who believes that Jesus is the Christ has been born of God" (1 John 5:1).[28]

Third, irresistible grace acknowledges the utter sovereignty of God's call. Christ's voice brought Lazarus from the grave, stilled the storm on the lake, and silenced and subdued the demons. Likewise, it is God's call in the gospel that brings us to salvation. Paul emphasized this, writing, "Those whom he predestined he also called, and those whom he called he also justified, and those whom he justified he also glorified" (Rom. 8:30). All of these are definitive and sovereign acts of God.

In this, we make a distinction between *synergism* and *monergism* in conversion. The prefix *syn* means "with" and *mono* means "alone." So synergism states that we cooperate with God in our conversion, whereas monergism ascribes conversion solely to God's sovereign grace. The example of Matthew, as well as those of Lydia, Peter, and many others, shows that conversion is monergistic. While we certainly are involved, everything we do in salvation results solely from God's sovereign and irresistible grace in our lives. Sproul elaborates:

> Monergistic regeneration is exclusively a divine act. Man does not have the creative power God has. To quicken a person who is spiritually dead is something only God can do. A corpse cannot revive itself. It cannot even assist in the effort. It can only respond after receiving new life. Not only can it respond then, it most certainly will respond.[29]

This leads to a fourth biblical defense of irresistible grace, namely, that life is always God's gift. The Bible describes our conversion to faith in Christ as God's gift of spiritual life. Paul wrote, "But God, being rich in mercy, because of the great love with which he loved us, even when we were dead in our trespasses, made us alive together with Christ—by grace you have been saved" (Eph. 2:4–5). When a sinner believes in Jesus, God has brought him or her to life. This is depicted in Jesus' call of Lazarus from the grave. Spiritually, we are no more able to act for our salvation than dead Lazarus could rise from his tomb. But Jesus called, "Lazarus, come out" (John 11:43), and the dead man came to life.

One objection to the doctrine of irresistible grace is that it supposedly involves a violation of our free wills. Some insist that God is a gentleman and would not press His will on an unwilling subject. Others have likened the effectual call to a spiritual rape. How do we respond to this? First, we can show that unless God's grace works within us without our prior permission, none of us would be saved. Moreover, God most certainly does not interact with us as a gentleman acts in polite society. God is the sovereign Lord. God is our Maker and Master. Thank God that He is not a gentleman when it comes to our salvation, lest He should stand by passively and permit us all to continue on our way to hell.

But it is especially appalling to describe God's sweet operation of grace in our salvation with the words *violence* or *rape*. God does not compel us to believe against our wills. Instead, He sovereignly changes our wills so that with new eyes we see Jesus as He is, with new hearts we embrace His salvation, and with new affections we love Him as the Savior of our souls. As the psalmist said, "Your people will offer themselves freely on the day of your power" (Ps. 110:3). This is the highest freedom: to have our souls brought to life so as to desire for ourselves that which is our greatest blessing and which brings the greatest glory to God through faith in Christ.

What's So Great about Irresistible Grace?

Our goal in these studies is not merely to learn the doctrines of grace, but to receive and experience the grace of the doctrines of grace. So while it is great to know what the Bible teaches about our salvation, it is better to know what is so great about the doctrines of grace. Therefore, let us ask, "What's so great about irresistible grace?"

The doctrine of irresistible grace is great primarily for the way it glorifies the saving work of the Holy Spirit and demonstrates the saving power of God's Word. The Spirit has been called the "shy" member of the Trinity because He always wants us to glorify Jesus Christ (see John 16:14). Yet like the other glorious persons of the Godhead, the Holy Spirit is worthy of the highest praise. It is especially by His irresistibly gracious working in our lives that the Spirit so merits our grateful worship.

Moreover, since irresistible grace reminds us that salvation is a supernatural work of God, it preserves us from deforming our ministries with man-made devices. For not only does irresistible grace glorify the Spirit as the sovereign agent of our conversion, it shows that the new birth results through the ministry of the Spirit-inspired Word of God. "You have been born again," Peter stated, "not of perishable seed but of imperishable, through the living and abiding word of God" (1 Peter 1:23). It is by effectually applying to our hearts the Scriptures that He brought into being that the Holy Spirit brings us to spiritual life. In this, His grace is highly exalted.

Indeed, irresistible grace glorifies the entire Trinity by proving how intimately involved God is in every conversion. It reminds us that when we speak about God's grace, we do not mean that God sits afar and cuts sinners a little slack by giving them a second chance. Rather, God places His holy hands on our filthy hearts. With more personal contact than any surgeon uses in operating on our bodies, God is intimately involved in saving our souls. How sublime beyond words it is to realize that the transcendent, majestic God takes such a personal interest in every sinner who comes to faith in Christ. Far from being a nameless number in a vast crowd, every believer has been personally ministered to by God's overwhelming grace. Truly, He is to us as a Father to His dear children and as a Shepherd to His beloved flock.

Furthermore, as the Bible describes it, irresistible grace is not a one-time encounter with God's power. Rather, conversion is only the beginning of a lifelong process of regeneration. When God takes away our stony hearts and gives us new and living hearts, He is hardly finished! Instead, He continues working in us and invites us lovingly to respond. Speaking of the Spirit's ministry in the new covenant age, God says, "I will put my laws into their minds, and write them on their hearts, and I will be their God, and they shall be my people" (Heb. 8:10). God's Spirit continues from our conversion to enlighten our minds with God's ways and to make our hearts tablets for His perfect law. It is certainly true that Christians can and do resist this process, but ultimately God's grace must and will achieve His intended result of bringing His people into perfect communion with His love. Despite all our sin and weakness, every Christian can know that God's irresistible grace destines us to partake of His glory. This means that Christians are granted power from God for the difficult life of faith. Paul prayed for the Ephesians, asking God that they might know "what is the immeasurable greatness of his power toward us who believe, according to the working of his great might that he worked in Christ when he raised him from the dead and seated him at his right hand in the heavenly places (Eph. 1:19–20).

The grace of the Spirit empowers us to know the love of Christ and experience the fullness of God. Later in Ephesians, Paul prayed that "according to the riches of his glory [God] may grant you to be strengthened with power through his Spirit in your inner being, so that Christ may dwell in your hearts through faith—that you . . . [may] know the love of Christ that surpasses knowledge, that you may be filled with all the fullness of God" (Eph. 3:16–19).

Finally, God's irresistible grace is great news not only for us, but also for others who have yet to come to Jesus. How can we really hope for hardened or uninterested sinners to trust in Jesus? By the same mighty grace by which we were saved.

Let this great teaching, then, embolden us in our witness and our service to others. Earlier, we noted that while the general call of Christ goes out to all the world, only the effectual call possesses power to save. But how this ennobles the general call, which God has now given us to proclaim. For it is through our feeble witness, offered generally to any and all who hear, that God irresistibly works to call more of His people to Himself. The power is all God's, as He sovereignly moves in this world by the Spirit. But the privilege is ours to be the voice that is heard, the hand that is felt, the prayer that is answered, and the witness that is used by God to bring eternal life. When sinners are saved through faith in Jesus, we have the joy of knowing that it is God who has acted irresistibly in grace through us.

6

What's So Great about the Perseverance of the Saints?

Philippians 1:6

✠ ✠ ✠

And I am sure of this, that he who began a good work in you will bring it to completion at the day of Jesus Christ. (Phil. 1:6)

John Duncan is regarded as one of the most holy men that Scotland produced in the nineteenth century. His vast learning in ancient languages earned him the nickname "Rabbi," but it was his fervent piety that earned the affection of the young men he helped prepare for the ministry. One former student remembered, "When we looked at 'the Rabbi' we all felt and were wont to say, 'There is the best evidence of Christianity, and especially the best evidence that there is such a thing as living personal godliness;

there is a man who walks closely with God, who actually knows what it is to enjoy the light of God's countenance.'"[30] Given this accolade, it may seem surprising that Duncan struggled throughout his life to gain assurance of salvation. A great deal of his spiritual energy was committed to anxiety over this issue. Would he persevere to the end in faith, he wondered? Concerns for this vital matter consumed much of Duncan's joy in life.

Rabbi Duncan was right to seek a proper foundation for his assurance of salvation. Surely all Christians experience anxiety over their future prospects for continuing in faith. It is for this reason that the doctrines of grace culminate with the doctrine of perseverance. Can believers in Jesus expect to persevere to the end so as to enter into glory, and if so, on what grounds?

It is appropriate for the five points of Calvinism to conclude with a matter of personal application. TULIP begins with man's problem: total depravity. It answers this problem with three gracious doctrines, each focused on a different person of the divine Trinity: the Father's unconditional election, the Son's limited atonement, and the Spirit's enlivening work of irresistible grace. We need now to return to the life of the believer to see how grace works out in practice. This is the issue with the P of TULIP: the perseverance of the saints.

The Perseverance of the Saints

The doctrine of the perseverance of the saints makes the simple point that those who are saved by grace must continue in faith until the end. The Bible is clear in stating that one is not saved merely on the basis of a dramatic conversion event that took place sometime in the past. Many professing Christians today are relying on the fact that they walked down the aisle during a revival service or that they prayed the sinner's prayer with their mothers when they were little. Such people will be alarmed to read what the Bible really says about our need to persevere in faith.

The New Testament contains a number of "if" statements regarding salvation that insist a past conversion event is not enough to assure us of salvation. Paul wrote to the Colossians in praise of the great saving work of Christ. Jesus died to bring reconciliation between heaven and earth, he wrote, "making peace by the blood of his cross" (Col. 1:20). This salvation had been experienced by the Christians at Colossae: "And you, who once were alienated and hostile in mind, doing evil deeds, he has now reconciled in his body of flesh by his death, in order to present you holy and blameless and above reproach before him" (Col. 1:21–22). These are beloved affirmations, but they are followed by a condition that is dreaded by many believing hearts: "if indeed you continue in the faith, stable and steadfast, not shifting from the hope of the gospel that you heard" (Col. 1:23). The dreaded "if"! With that word, it seems to many that salvation has descended from the realm of God's grace back to the burdensome world of human ability and attainments.

Lest we should think Paul's "if" statement represents a momentary lapse on the apostle's part from the doctrines of grace, the Bible has plenty of other verses to keep the fearful Christian awake at night. The writer of Hebrews warns us, "Take care, brothers, lest there be in any of you an evil, unbelieving heart, leading you to fall away from the living God" (Heb. 3:12). The apostle Peter exhorts his readers to "be all the more diligent to make your calling and election sure" (2 Peter 1:10). Jesus is most direct: "The one who endures to the end will be saved" (Matt. 10:22). The book of Revelation includes numerous statements to this effect. The theme of that whole book may be summed up with the words of 14:12: "Here is a call for the endurance of the saints, those who keep the commandments of God and their faith in Jesus."

These biblical teachings put a distinct color on an oft-heard statement: "Once saved, always saved." This is a true statement when rightly understood. But wrongly understood—or rather wrongly presumed on—it can lead to a tragic assumption. Yes, those who are once saved are always saved—but only by persevering in the faith and in obedience to Christ.

As in most doctrinal matters, John Bunyan's great book, *The Pilgrim's Progress,* yields a helpful illustration. Bunyan's hero, Christian, is saved in dramatic fashion. Living in the City of Destruction, he comes under conviction of sin and fear of judgment, and flees for his life. Being directed to the gospel by Evangelist, he heads for the narrow gate to salvation, which leads to the cross. It is there at the cross that Christian loses the burden of his sin, which falls from his back. Saved through faith alone, he is ministered to by three "Shining Ones." The first one proclaims the forgiveness of his sins. The second removes his filthy rags and dresses him in robes of righteousness. The third puts a mark on his forehead and gives him a sealed scroll, a certificate that he can present at the gates of the Celestial City to gain entry into its glory.[31] What a lovely and helpful portrayal of what it means to be "once saved"! At the cross of Christ—and there only—faith receives full forgiveness of all sins, the imputed righteousness of Christ, and the seal of salvation to eternal life. Once saved! The sinner who looks in faith to the cross of Christ has his past redeemed and his future secured.

Yet we should note that *The Pilgrim's Progress* does not end with the scene at the cross. Neither is Christian translated immediately to the Celestial City, there to present his passport and enter. The scene at the cross is early in the book, just as conversion to faith in Christ is at the beginning of a person's life journey of faith. There is much for Christian yet to face—and face it he must. There are hills to climb, temptations to overcome, dragons to be fought, and trials to be endured. For the certificate of salvation received at the cross cannot be faxed to heaven or emailed to the heavenly server. It must be hand-delivered. When Christian arrives at the gates of the city, he must still have the certificate of his faith in hand, or else his entry will be denied. To get there he must conquer, prevail, and endure through obedience to God and His Word. In Christian's salvation, these two go together: the narrow gate of the cross and the pilgrim's path that leads to heaven. Revelation 14:12 is right: this calls for "the endurance of the saints, those who keep the commandments of God and their faith in Jesus."

Where to Look for Assurance

So far in our consideration of this doctrine we have the curious situation of the Arminian and the Calvinist in full agreement: the saints of God must persevere in faith in order to be saved. Iain Murray recounts an iron-sharpening conversation on this subject between a Calvinist theologian and a Wesleyan Methodist teacher. The Calvinist asked, "Do you believe in the perseverance of saints?" When the Arminian teacher answered, "Certainly," the Calvinist expressed surprise. "I thought you did not," he replied. "O, Sir, you have been misinformed," the Methodist preacher replied. "It is the perseverance of sinners we doubt."[32] If by "sinners" the Wesleyan meant professing sinners who continue living in the way of sin, he was right, and on this Calvinists and Arminians are in fact agreed.

But the agreement ends there. For the subject of perseverance proceeds directly to an important matter over which the two sides fall into sharp disagreement. The question has to do with the certainty of a true Christian persevering, or to put it differently, the possibility of a true believer falling away. Can a genuinely saved person, a man or woman who has truly come to faith in Jesus, lose that salvation by failing to persevere? The Arminian answers, "Yes," whereas the Calvinist answers, "No." Both agree that those once saved must continue to be saved through an enduring faith. But while the Arminian states that perseverance is possible but not certain, the Calvinist asserts that for a true Christian perseverance is sure.

It was uncertainty over this issue that plagued the soul of

Rabbi Duncan in nineteenth-century Scotland. It was two years after his conversion to faith in Christ before Duncan was strongly convicted of the reality of his sin. During these two years, he lived loosely, both in doctrine and in life. When he fully realized God's hatred of sin, it had a shattering effect on his assurance. Thereafter, his biographer recounts: "Dr. Duncan was ever suspicious of his own heart and was hard on himself. . . . [He had] a very high view of what it meant to be a Christian, and this together with his own suspicion of himself was undoubtedly at the root of some of his difficulties."[33]

For all the profundity of his theological learning, and for all the evidence of grace seen in him by others, Duncan looked constantly into his own heart and saw alarming signs. He saw the existence of lusts and a brewing cauldron of sins. He saw an insufficient zeal for Christ and an unworthy pride. He acknowledged to friends that he was often in "a legal state." By this he meant that he sought assurance of salvation and hope for perseverance in the reality and potential of his own spiritual performance. He wrote of one sleepless night, one of a great many he endured: "I was in terrible agony last night at the thought of a Christless state, and that I might be in it. The fear of it exhausted my faculties. I had a flickering hope."[34]

How are we to assess Duncan's situation? According to the Arminian scheme, his fears were well-founded, if overly morbid. One must persevere in godliness, and should therefore respond to signs of existing sin with a fearful resolve. Arminian assurance of salvation comes through finding proof of regeneration, and at this Rabbi Duncan could not succeed. His private writings are cluttered with questions about the state of his soul. Unable to affirm from self-examination that his soul was regenerate, he wrote, "I fear I may be in hell yet."[35]

What is the Calvinist response to this? The great difference is that the Reformed doctrine of perseverance calls for the Christian to look not to himself for assurance of salvation but to God and His promises in Christ. While a laxity concerning sin is to be loathed, the presence of sin in our hearts is only to be expected. Even Paul confessed, "Not that I have already obtained this or am already perfect, but I press on to make it my own, because Christ Jesus has made me his own" (Phil. 3:12). So we look not to ourselves for perseverance, but to the faithful God's sovereign, preserving grace.

That this is the biblical doctrine of perseverance may be seen in many passages, but perhaps most clearly in Paul's teaching in Philippians 1:6. While Arminians and Calvinists agree that a saint must persevere in salvation, who is the principal agent of my perseverance? Is perseverance something that occurs by my activity, though with the help of God? Or do Christians persevere by God's activity, though certainly with the full involvement of the believer? Paul answers, "I am sure of this, that he who began a good work in you will bring it to completion at the day of Jesus Christ."

God's Promise of Preserving Grace

The New Testament provides numerous answers to the question of how a believer may hope to persevere. John 5:24 speaks of the definite transition when a person genuinely believes in Christ: "Whoever hears my word and believes him who sent me has eternal life. He does not come into judgment, but has passed from death to life." Likewise, in Romans 11:29, Paul insists that God's gift of eternal life is indeed eternal: "the gifts and the calling of God are irrevocable." Jesus promises eternal security for His purchased sheep, who are marked by a living faith: "I give them eternal life, and they will never perish, and no one will snatch them out of my hand" (John 10:28). And Peter directs a believer's hope to "an inheritance that is imperishable, undefiled, and unfading, kept in heaven for you, who by God's power are being guarded through faith for a salvation ready to be revealed in the last time" (1 Peter 1:4–5).

Along these lines, Philippians 1:6 develops the theme of God's preserving grace—which ensures the perseverance of His own—in three points. The first is Paul's reminder that since God has begun our salvation, we can rely on Him to complete it: "he who began a good work in you will bring it to completion." God always finishes what He starts, especially the salvation of His people.

It is in this way that God's preserving grace fits with the other doctrines of grace. God the Father chose us in eternity past, and the Bible says that God's purpose in election must prevail (Rom. 9:11). God the Son offered an atoning sacrifice for these same elect people. Should they fall into condemnation, then His blood would have been shed for them in vain. But He insists that not one of them shall perish and none shall be plucked from His hand (John 10:28). Likewise, the Holy Spirit brought these same elect sheep to eternal life by the irresistible working of His grace. Should eternal life be lost, the Spirit's work would prove ineffective. Therefore, as faith is the gift of God's grace, the Christian's perseverance is the work of God's continuing grace.

Notice, secondly, that Paul says that God, having begun His work in our lives, "will bring it" to completion. This indicates that God not only guarantees the completion of our salvation, but is actively involved in the believer's life to bring this to pass. God works in our lives in the way a craftsman works to finish a product he has created. He smooths out the lines, sands the rough places, and puts its pieces together in proper proportion. D. Martyn Lloyd-Jones writes:

> God does not merely initiate the work and then leave it, he continues with it; he leads us on, directing and manipulating our circumstances, restraining us at one time and urging us on at another. Paul's whole conception of the Church is that it is a place where God is working in the hearts of men and women.[36]

God's work is manifested in His will playing out in our lives. This is what Paul says a bit later in Philippians: "Work out your own salvation with fear and trembling, for it is God who works in you, both to will and to work for his good pleasure" (Phil. 2:12–13). Being a Christian is not easy. Persevering in faith requires warfare with sin, labor in prayer, plowing in God's Word, and performing His will in the world. We are God's workmanship, Paul says, and this means we are called to "good works, which

God prepared beforehand, that we should walk in them" (Eph. 2:10). God will see to it that His work for each of us is carried to completion. By His preserving grace, He will carry us to our destination in heaven. We are called to work this out, but, Paul insists, God is all the while working it in us (Phil. 2:13).

This leads to the third great point we can see in Philippians 1:6, namely, our certainty of successful "completion" if God's saving work truly has begun in us. Far from dreading the future, as we must if we look for signs of hope within ourselves, every believer possesses a hope that is certain for the most joyful, glorious, and holy destiny through faith in Jesus.

One of the reasons I love Bunyan's *The Pilgrim's Progress* is the portrait he paints of the eternity God has secured for every believer. Speaking of the believer's entry into heaven, he writes:

> I saw in my dream the two men enter the gate. As they did, they were transfigured. They had garments that shined like gold. Harps and crowns were given them. The harps for praise and the crowns for honor. Then I heard in my dream all the bells in the city rang again for joy. It was said to them, "Enter into the joy of your Lord."[37]

This may be a fanciful rendering from the Bible's promises, but still it is our future history and not fantasy. For as Paul insists, God brings us to completion. One of the meanings of the Greek word translated as "bring to completion" is "bring to perfection." That is what God has promised to do for every sheep who hears Christ's voice and who shows the reality of his or her faith by following after Him through life. Whatever hardships, disappointments, or failures await us in this world, a Christian can anticipate the certain fulfillment of David's exultant words in Psalm 16:11: "You make known to me the path of life; in your presence there is fullness of joy; at your right hand are pleasures forevermore." Terribly flawed though we all are now, God will bring our journey to completion and us to perfection, so that arrayed in perfect holiness we will live forever in His love.

What's So Great about the Perseverance of the Saints?

If only Rabbi Duncan had settled his heart on these truths, his misery might have turned to joy. He believed in Jesus and was saved, but he looked to himself for his future hope and was thus overwhelmed with anxiety. Paul would have us look instead to God for the whole of our salvation. Knowing that our faith is born of God's electing grace, let us leave our whole case in those sovereign hands. Looking to Christ for the forgiveness of our sins, let us never remove our gaze from the emblem of His love that is the cross. Having felt the irresistible working of the Holy Spirit in our hearts, let us leave off all resistance, keeping in step with His leading in anticipation of God's further work in our lives.

This is the chief benefit of the Bible's doctrine of perseverance: it is a call to rely wholly on God's preserving grace, since He has promised to complete what He has begun. This may be even more important for maturing Christians than for new converts.

For the more we progress in our walk with God, the deeper sense we have of our sin. This sense of sin must be accompanied by a growing knowledge of God's faithfulness, power, and love.

This knowledge of God is gained through a life of regular devotion with the Lord. Here we may discover a key to Duncan's problem. Duncan was a linguistic genius, and most of his study was directed toward a more exhaustive and precise knowledge of numerous languages. He led a disordered life, often absorbing himself in technical studies all night. He admitted that his academic work often left little time for the devotional study of Scripture and for prayer. Surely this neglect must have played a role in the loosening of his grip on the graciousness of God's salvation. His struggles warn us with regard to all of the work we are called to do for Christ: if we are to feel the effects of our faith, our service must never replace the personal life of the soul in fellowship with its Savior.

Lastly, an awareness of God's present grace—His grace for the journey as well as for its beginning and end—should elevate our hopes for daily joy. This is what's so great about the perseverance of the saints: the certainty believers have at all times that God is graciously working for our salvation.

Perhaps, for instance, a grace-centered believer falls into a sin. Instead of being undone by inward doubts and questions regarding his or her salvation, the believer should ask how God is using this failure for his or her sanctification. I might ask, is God revealing my overconfidence in the flesh and my need to rely more closely on His Word? Is God preparing me for a future challenge, so that I will not fail then? Is God humbling me or showing me a particular vulnerability? The answer is probably somewhere along these lines. But what a liberating difference it makes to view life in terms of God's certain success instead of in terms of our inevitable failure!

The doctrine of God's preserving grace may be even more important in the event of our success and spiritual achievement. Instead of glorying in ourselves, to which we all are prone— "Look what I have done!"—we glory in God's faithfulness and might. We celebrate what God is doing in us and draw nearer to Him instead of puffing up with self-reliance that can only draw us away from the spring of God's flowing grace.

In either case—failure or success—possessing a firm confidence in God's preserving grace makes all the difference now. Are you a believer in Christ? Then realize that this is a work of grace begun in you by God. What He has begun, He is certain to bring to completion and perfection!

Remember Bunyan's portrait of the saints' entry into glory— the flags of heaven rippling, angelic trumpets blaring, the golden gates of glory opening wide? The far greater reality awaiting us is a certain experience in our future. Knowing this, is it not easier to live as a citizen of heaven, though still in this world?

Perhaps you are burdened with troubles and trials. Many Christians are. Yet you still have every reason to rejoice, for you are chosen of God, blood-bought by the Son, and sealed by the Spirit for an eternity of glory. "Rejoice in the Lord always," Paul therefore concludes. "Again I will say, Rejoice" (Phil. 4:4). Perhaps you are poor, yet in Christ you can know that a glorious inheritance is laid up for you (1 Peter 1:4). Perhaps you are sick or even dying. But you can know that "What is sown is perishable; what is raised is imperishable" (1 Cor. 15:42). The salvation God has begun in you, He will complete! Those whom God has caused to be born again, He will bring to glorious perfection! Knowing and rejoicing in God's preserving, completing, and perfecting grace will enable you to lay down your head in peace at night and rise up energized to live for God in joy each day.

So Great a God of Grace

Summing up all the doctrines of grace, this is what's so great: those who know and rely on God's all-sufficient grace—the grace of the Father, the grace of the Son, and the grace of the Holy Spirit—are inspired to live for His all-consuming glory. There's nothing greater than that. For our greatest joy is found in fulfilling our highest purpose, and our highest purpose is to live for the praise of our all-glorious God of grace. To Him be glory, both now and forever, through His grace at work in us.

NOTES

1   R. C. Sproul, *The Holiness of God* (Wheaton, Ill.: Tyndale House, 1990), 32.

2   Cited in Ravi Zacharias, *Can Man Live Without God?* (Dallas, Texas: Word, 1994), 137.

3   Francis A. Schaeffer, *The Francis A. Schaeffer Trilogy: Three Essential Books in One Volume* (Wheaton, Ill.: Crossway Books, 1990), 135.

4   Loraine Boettner, *The Reformed Doctrine of Predestination* (Phillipsburg, N.J.: P&R Publishing, 1963), 61.

5   Arthur W. Pink, *The Sovereignty of God* (Grand Rapids, Mich.: Baker Books, 1930, reprint 1993), 136.

6   Francis A. Schaeffer, *The Finished Work of Christ* (Wheaton, Ill.: Crossway Books, 1998), 70.

7   John Calvin, *Institutes of the Christian Religion*, *Library of Christian Classics*, John T. McNeill, ed.; Ford Lewis Battles, trans. (Philadelphia, Pa.: Westminster Press, 1960), 1:XI, 108.

8   D. Martyn Lloyd-Jones, *The Cross* (Wheaton, Ill.: Crossway Books, 1986), 118.

9   George Bennard, "The Old Rugged Cross," 1913.

10   Jerry Walls, "An Interview with Jerry Walls," *Modern Reformation*, Vol. 15, No. 5, Sept/Oct. 2006, 28.

11   Donald Grey Barnhouse, *Expositions on the Whole Bible Using the Book of Romans as a Point of Departure,* 10 vols. (Grand Rapids, Mich.: Eerdmans Publishing, 1963), 8:38.

12   Pink, *The Sovereignty of God*, 218–19.

13   John Calvin, *The Mystery of Godliness and Other Sermons* (Morgan, Pa.: Soli Deo Gloria, 1830, reprint 1990), 87.

14 James Montgomery Boice, "Alive in Christ," *Hymns for a Modern Reformation* (Philadelphia, Pa.: Tenth Presbyterian Church, 2000), 25.

15 Cited in Philip Graham Ryken, *The Sovereignty of God's Mercy* (Greenville, S.C.: Reformed Academic Press, 2001), 16–17.

16 Bruce Demarest, *The Cross and Salvation* (Wheaton, Ill.: Crossway Books, 1997), 191, 193.

17 John Owen, *The Death of Death in the Death of Christ* (Edinburgh, Scotland, and Carlisle, Pa.: Banner of Truth Trust, 1959), 302.

18 John Murray, *Redemption Accomplished and Applied* (Grand Rapids, Mich.: Eerdmans Publishing, 1955), 63–64.

19 J. I. Packer, "Introductory Essay," in Owen, *The Death of Death in the Death of Christ*, 12.

20 James Montgomery Boice and Philip Graham Ryken, *The Doctrines of Grace* (Wheaton, Ill.: Crossway Books, 2002), 120.

21 Murray, *Redemption Accomplished and Applied*, 75.

22 Owen, *The Death of Death in the Death of Christ*, 123.

23 Ibid., 137.

24 Packer, "Introductory Essay," in Owen, *The Death of Death in the Death of Christ*, 12.

25 John Murray, "The Assurance of Faith," in *Collected Writings of John Murray*, 4 vols. (Edinburgh, Scotland, and Carlisle, Pa.: Banner of Truth Trust, 1977), 2:266–267.

26 R. C. Sproul, *The Mystery of the Holy Spirit* (Wheaton, Ill.: Tyndale House, 1994), 110

27 Murray, *Redemption Accomplished and Applied*, 96.

28 Sadly, most English translations do not render this verse accurately, stating instead, "Whoever believes that Jesus is the Christ *is born* of God." But the Greek text is unambiguous in its use of the perfect tense: "*has been born* of God." Rebirth precedes faith.

29 R. C. Sproul, *What Is Reformed Theology?* (Grand Rapids, Mich.: Baker Books, 1997), 184.

30 Cited in John E. Marshall, "Rabbi Duncan and the Problem of Assurance," in *Life and Writings* (Edinburgh, Scotland, and Carlisle, Pa.: Banner of Truth Trust, 2005), 207.

31 John Bunyan, *The Pilgrim's Progress* (Nashville, Tenn.: Thomas Nelson, 1999), 35–36.

32 Cited in Iain Murray, *Wesley and Men Who Followed* (Edinburgh, Scotland, and Carlisle, Pa.: Banner of Truth Trust, 2003), 66.

33 Marshall, *Life and Writings*, 218, 222–223.

34 Ibid., 205.

35 Ibid., 203.

36 D. Martyn Lloyd-Jones, *The Life of Joy* (Grand Rapids, Mich.: Baker Books, 1989), 38.

37 Bunyan, *The Pilgrim's Progress*, 136–37.

Index of Scripture

Index of Subjects and Names

About the Author

RICHARD D. PHILLIPS (M.Div., Westminster Theological Seminary) is senior minister of the historic Second Presbyterian Church in Greenville, S.C. He is the author of numerous books, including *Jesus the Evangelist* and *Hebrews* in the Reformed Expository Commentary series. His preaching is heard weekly on the radio program *God's Living Word*, and since 2000 he has chaired the Philadelphia Conference on Reformed Theology, founded by James Montgomery Boice. Prior to his calling to the gospel ministry, Rev. Phillips served as a tank officer in the U.S. Army and was assistant professor of leadership at the United States Military Academy, West Point, resigning with the rank of major. He lives with his wife, Sharon, and their five children in the Upcountry of South Carolina.